LOUIS B. WRIGHT, General Editor. Director of the Folger Shakespeare Library from 1948 until his retirement in 1968, Dr. Wright has devoted over forty years to the study of the Shakespearean period. In 1926 he completed his doctoral thesis on "Vaudeville Elements in Elizabethan Drama" and subsequently published many articles on the stagecraft and theatre of Shakespeare's day. He is the author of *Middle-Class Culture in Elizabethan England* (1935), *Religion and Empire* (1942), *The Elizabethans' America* (1965), and many other books and essays on the history and literature of the Tudor and Stuart periods, including *Shakespeare for Everyman* (1964). Dr. Wright has taught at the universities of North Carolina, California at Los Angeles, Michigan, Minnesota, and other American institutions. From 1932 to 1948 he was instrumental in developing the research program of the Henry E. Huntington Library and Art Gallery. During his tenure as Director, the Folger Shakespeare Library became one of the leading research institutions of the world for the study of the backgrounds of Anglo-American civilization.

VIRGINIA A. LaMAR, Assistant Editor. A member of the staff of the Folger Shakespeare Library from 1946 until her death in 1968, Miss LaMar served as research assistant to the Director and as Executive Secretary. Prior to 1946 Miss LaMar had been a secretary in the British Admiralty Delegation in Washington, D.C., receiving the King's Medal in 1945 for her services. She was coeditor of the *Historie of Travell into Virginia Britania* by William Strachey, published by The Hakluyt Society in 1953, and author of *English Dress in the Age of Shakespeare* and *Travel and Roads in England* in the "Folger Booklets on Tudor and Stuart Civilization" series.

The Folger Shakespeare Library

The Folger Shakespeare Library in Washington, D.C., a research institute founded and endowed by Henry Clay Folger and administered by the Trustees of Amherst College, contains the world's largest collection of Shakespeareana. Although the Folger Library's primary purpose is to encourage advanced research in history and literature, it has continually exhibited a profound concern in stimulating a popular interest in the Elizabethan period.

A complete brochure of the materials produced under the guidance of Louis B. Wright and Virginia A. LaMar—texts of the plays, supplementary reading, and recordings—is available free on request from Washington Square Press, a division of Simon & Schuster, Inc., Educational Department, 630 Fifth Avenue, New York, N.Y. 10020.

GENERAL EDITOR

LOUIS B. WRIGHT
Director, Folger Shakespeare Library, 1948–1968

•

ASSISTANT EDITOR

VIRGINIA A. LaMAR
Executive Secretary, Folger Shakespeare Library, 1946–1968

The Folger Library General Reader's Shakespeare

A MIDSUMMER NIGHT'S DREAM

By

WILLIAM
SHAKESPEARE

WASHINGTON SQUARE PRESS
POCKET BOOKS • NEW YORK

A MIDSUMMER NIGHT'S DREAM

WASHINGTON SQUARE PRESS edition published August, 1958
21st printing...................September, 1975

A new edition of a distinguished
literary work now made available in
an inexpensive, well-designed format

Published by
POCKET BOOKS, a division of Simon & Schuster, Inc.,
630 Fifth Avenue, New York, N.Y.

WASHINGTON SQUARE PRESS editions are distrib-
uted in the U.S. by Simon & Schuster, Inc., 630 Fifth
Avenue, New York, N.Y. 10020, and in Canada by Simon
& Schuster of Canada, Ltd., Markham, Ontario, Canada.

Standard Book Number: 671-48161-4.

Preface

This edition of *A Midsummer Night's Dream* is designed to make available a readable text of one of Shakespeare's most popular plays. In the centuries since Shakespeare many changes have occurred in the meanings of words, and some clarification of Shakespeare's vocabulary may be helpful. To provide the reader with necessary notes in the most accessible format, we have placed them on the pages facing the text that they explain. We have tried to make these notes as brief and simple as possible. Preliminary to the text we have also included a brief statement of essential information about Shakespeare and his stage. Readers desiring more detailed information should refer to the books suggested in the references, and if still further information is needed, the bibliographies in those books will provide the necessary clues to the literature of the subject.

The early texts of all of Shakespeare's plays provide only inadequate stage directions, and it is conventional for modern editors to add many that clarify the action. Such additions, and additions to entrances, are placed in square brackets.

All illustrations are from material in the Folger Library collections.

L. B. W.
V. A. L.

February 1, 1958

A Fairy Fantasy

A Midsummer Night's Dream is one of Shakespeare's most popular comedies and has long been a favorite for amateur production, especially on the campuses of women's colleges, where Titania, Oberon, Puck, and the other fairies are wont to frisk and frolic about Commencement time. The play has the lilt and spirit of youth, and the romantic poetry has the freshness and fragrance of spring flowers. The time of its action is not midsummer, as the title might suggest, but about May Day, and the title merely alludes to the gay madness proverbially associated with the rites of Midsummer's Eve, or those of May Day, for that matter. The play is a fantasy of folklore and fairies, a medley of poetry, song, and dance, with vivid contrasts between the dainty folk in Titania's train and the "rude mechanicals" in Bottom's company. It has some of the qualities of the masque, a favorite form of light entertainment at court or at celebrations in the houses of the nobility.

Internal evidence indicates that Shakespeare wrote *A Midsummer Night's Dream* for the wedding of some great personage, but that personage's identity has escaped literary historians. Scholars have guessed that it might have been written for the wedding of William

Stanley, Earl of Derby, and Elizabeth Vere, daughter of the Earl of Oxford, which took place in the presence of Queen Elizabeth at her palace at Greenwich on January 26, 1595. An elaborate compliment to the Queen in Act II, Scene i, the "fair Vestal, throned by the West," suggests that she was present when the play was first presented. Since other references make 1595 seem a likely date for the production of the play, the Earl of Derby's wedding is at least a possible occasion.

The masque was a favorite type of entertainment for such occasions, and *A Midsummer Night's Dream* is Shakespeare's nearest approach to that form of spectacle in which Ben Jonson became a master. In a book entitled *The Court Masque,* Miss Enid Welsford suggests the relations between regular drama and the masque: "The drama is a story with crisis and dénouement; the masque is an invention moving upon a hinge, or, to put it another way, it is the logical working out of an idea which has to be taken for granted. The hinge of a masque was as a rule some riddling compliment of the sovereign, or an actual event, which was represented as taking place in Olympus or Arcadia, or as being so magnificent an affair that divinities were brought down to celebrate it" (p. 256). The masque was an elaborate show that emphasized spectacular elements, costume, and scenic devices rather than dramatic plot and poetry. Music, dancing, and pageantry were its concomitants. Normally it had allegorical figures—gods, goddesses, shepherds, shepherdesses, and other creatures of fancy beautifully costumed who sang, danced, and paraded before the guests. These creations had as foils a contrasting group known as the antimasque, who might be anything from satyrs to earthy yokels comically attired.

The similarity of *A Midsummer Night's Dream* to the spirit of the masque is obvious, but as always in Shakespeare, his genius transcends conventions, and he writes a poetic drama instead of a stereotyped pageant. And with consummate skill he weaves three separate elements of the play together to give it unity. The main plot concerns the wedding of Theseus and Hippolyta and the love story of Lysander, Demetrius, Hermia, and Helena. To provide entertainment at the wedding, the Athenian artisans plan to give the play of Pyramus and Thisby. The story of the quarrel of Oberon and Titania and of the activities of the fairies parallels the main plot; but by making Puck the instrument for solving the problems of the earthly lovers and increasing the confusions and comedy of the artisans, the author brings the groups together in an organic whole.

Although our main interest may be in the fairy passages and the burlesque humor of the artisans, *A Midsummer Night's Dream* is not merely an entertaining spectacle like any number of masques that endured for a night and long since have been forgotten. Shakespeare always provides a meaning and a significance deeper than the surface ripples of mere entertainment. His plays are filled with commentary on life and love, and in this play from his early period, he treats the whimsical and irresponsible aspects of love, the midsummer madness that has no explanation except the whims of men and women or the deviltry of Robin Goodfellow. But Shakespeare contemplates these moods and qualities in no spirit of criticism or reproof. Love can make men and women do many foolish things, but the author and his audience laugh gaily at such folly and accept it as the norm of life. "Lord, what fools these mortals be!" Puck exclaims, but, for all of that, mortals are rather charming beings, at least on this "wedding day at night," and neither Puck nor Shakespeare shows any desire to change them. Written for a happy occasion, the play touches lightly on problems of love and marriage that receive more profound treatment in *Romeo and Juliet* and later plays.

As was suitable in an entertainment designed for a wedding, the play closes with an epithalamium as the fairies flit about doing good and making amends for any confusions they may have caused before. Oberon, now in full control of his own fairy household, gives orders:

> Now, until the break of day,
> Through this house each fairy stray.
> To the best bride-bed will we,
> Which by us shall blessed be;
> And the issue there create
> Ever shall be fortunate.

And Puck, reformed and repentant after his gay trickeries, comments:

> If we shadows have offended,
> Think but this, and all is mended—
> That you have but slumb'red here
> While these visions did appear.

Thus the play ends and the wedding guests troop home humming softly one of the fairy airs.

In his treatment of the fairies, Shakespeare departed

from traditional folklore to give them a benignity that they did not always possess. Shakespeare's age believed in witches, hobgoblins, and ghosts, and to the average countryman of Warwickshire fairies connoted devils and hobgoblins rather than the "little people." Though Shakespeare's Puck might be a "shrewd and knavish sprite," playing tricks on housewives and night wanderers, he was not the terrifying Hobgoblin of popular fancy, and ever after Shakespeare he would have a disposition and a nature vastly improved. Indeed, Shakespeare's imaginative concept of the fairies as dainty beings of gauze and gossamer influenced most of the fairy literature that came after him.

The sources of *A Midsummer Night's Dream* are scattered and diverse, derived from reading here and there, and indeed in part from oral tradition. The love story of Theseus and Hippolyta he may have remembered from Chaucer's *Knight's Tale,* and he may have found facts about Theseus in Sir Thomas North's translation of *Plutarch's Lives* (1579). The tale of Pyramus and Thisby is in Ovid's *Metamorphoses* and in Chaucer's *Legend of Good Women.* Various other bits and pieces in the play may have come from his desultory reading. A professional writer is likely to tuck away in his memory a wide variety of oddments that he will use at some later time.

The fairy lore is both traditional and literary in its sources. Tales of goblins and sprites were common enough, and Shakespeare could have heard about Robin Goodfellow from his nurse. Oberon, as king of the fairies, had already appeared in Spenser's *Faerie Queene* and elsewhere. Robert Greene, in a play *James the Fourth* (*ca.* 1591), had employed Oberon as a character. The source for the name Titania is not clear. For such sprites as Cobweb and Peaseblossom, Shakespeare had only to search his own imagination.

For the artisans, Shakespeare drew on his own memory of yokels and craftsmen he had known at Stratford or had observed in the byways of London. Bottom, the weaver, Quince, the carpenter, Flute, the bellows-mender, and all the rest may have been domiciled in Athens but they are authentically English, and the humor is the robust humor that comes from intimate contact with simple folk. However closely people may live in cities, the countryman and small townsman usually acquire a more accurate understanding of the vagaries of human nature, and they almost always possess a keener capacity for observation, than the city dweller. No city slicker could have created Bottom—or Falstaff. The humor of witty byplay and the wisecrack may emanate from urban sophisticates, but the humor that originates in the idiosyncrasies of human nature, particularly the earthy humor illustrated by the Bottoms and the Falstaffs, is likely to have its source in the mind of one who has observed closely the people who make up the population of the small town and the countryside.

HISTORY OF THE PLAY

A Midsummer Night's Dream has had a long and interesting stage history. How great was its popularity when Shakespeare's company performed it in the playhouse, the records do not show, but the title page of the First Quarto, printed in 1600, declared that it had been "sundry times publicly acted." In 1598, Francis

Meres, a young preacher, in a volume called *Palladis Tamia: Wits Treasury*, listed it among the comedies for which Shakespeare was famed. We know of a performance on Sunday, September 27, 1631, in the house of John Williams, Bishop of Lincoln. The Puritans made an uproar because a bishop had allowed a heathen play to be performed on his premises on a Sunday.

During the period after 1642 when the Puritans kept the theatres closed, a short skit, or droll as it was called, based on the artisans' parts appears to have been acted in private. This droll was printed in 1661, and again in 1672, as *The Merry Conceited Humors of Bottom the Weaver*. It enjoyed considerable popularity and was even performed in Germany.

After the Restoration of Charles II, *A Midsummer Night's Dream* was one of the Shakespearean plays that had a revival. Samuel Pepys saw it at the King's Theatre on September 29, 1662, and commented in his *Diary* that it was "the most insipid ridiculous play that ever I saw in my life." In 1692 Henry Purcell, one of the great composers and musicians of the period, prepared an operatic version of the play with the title *The Fairy Queen*, which was produced at Dorset Garden. In 1716 Richard Leveridge, another musician, made a burlesque of Italian opera out of the artisans' portions of the play. This piece enjoyed considerable popularity as an afterpiece, a comic bit performed at the end of any full-length play. In 1723 Charles Johnson made an adaptation from *As You Like It* called *Love in a Forest* and gilded the lily by adding in the last act a portion of the Pyramus and Thisby episode from *A Midsummer Night's Dream*. Various other adaptations were seen during the eighteenth and early nineteenth centuries. David Garrick put on a version at Drury Lane that left out the artisans, who violated his sense of decorum and propriety.

While English performances were still being given in abbreviated and garbled versions, the great German Shakespearean Ludwig Tieck in 1827 revived Shakespeare's true text for a performance in Berlin. For this performance, Mendelssohn composed music that has endured in popularity from that day to this. From the mid-nineteenth century onward, the play has been performed for the most part as Shakespeare wrote it, but in the 1930's Max Reinhardt staged a performance at Los Angeles, California, in the Hollywood Bowl, that outdid anything in the eighteenth century for pretentious nonsense. The hillside back of the Hollywood Bowl was strung with electric wires so that thousands of blue lights signifying fairies could glow and flicker at the proper time. Three hundred wedding guests carrying lighted flambeaux wound down from the hills to take part in the play. Reinhardt's motion-picture version was planned on the same scale, and the poetry of Shakespeare was lost in a wilderness of stage effects. Despite such occasional deviations from good taste, most modern productions have tried to retain the spirit of Shakespeare's theatre, and *A Midsummer Night's Dream* remains an important item in Shakespearean repertory theatres and is a frequent choice for amateur productions.

THE TEXT

A Midsummer Night's Dream was licensed for printing on October 8, 1600, and was printed in the same year with the title: *A Midsommer nights dreame. As it hath beene sundry times publickely acted, by the Right honourable, the Lord Chamberlaine his seruants. Written by William Shakespeare. Imprinted at London, for Thomas Fisher, and are to be soulde at his shoppe, at the Signe of the White Hart, in Fleetestreete. 1600.* This is known as the First Quarto. A Second Quarto "Printed by Iames Roberts, 1600," is a pirated edition of the First Quarto, but is falsely dated and was really printed in 1619. The next printing of the play was in the First Folio, the collected edition of 1623. The text of the First Quarto has relatively few errors and corruptions. The copy for the First Folio printing of the play appears to have been a corrected version of the Second Quarto, which may have been used as a prompt copy for a revival of the play in 1619. The present edition is based on the First Quarto with corrections suggested by variant readings in the First Folio.

THE AUTHOR

As EARLY AS 1598 Shakespeare was so well known as a literary and dramatic craftsman that Francis Meres, in his *Palladis Tamia: Wits Treasury,* referred in flattering terms to him as "mellifluous and honey-tongued Shakespeare," famous for his *Venus and Adonis,* his *Lucrece,* and "his sugared sonnets," which were circulating "among his private friends." Meres observes further that "as Plautus and Seneca are accounted the best for comedy and tragedy among the Latins, so Shakespeare among the English is the most excellent in both kinds for the stage," and he mentions a dozen plays that had made a name for Shakespeare. He concludes with the remark "that the Muses would speak with Shakespeare's fine filed phrase if they would speak English."

To those acquainted with the history of the Elizabethan and Jacobean periods, it is incredible that anyone should be so naïve or ignorant as to doubt the reality of Shakespeare as the author of the plays that bear his name. Yet so much nonsense has been written about other "candidates" for the plays that it is well to remind readers that no credible evidence that would stand up in a court of law has ever been adduced to prove either that Shakespeare did not write his plays or that anyone else wrote them. All the theories offered for the authorship of Francis Bacon, the Earl of Derby, the Earl of Oxford, the Earl of Hertford, Christopher Marlowe, and a score of other candidates are mere conjectures spun from the active imaginations of persons who confuse hypothesis and conjecture with evidence.

As Meres' statement of 1598 indicates, Shakespeare was already a popular playwright whose name carried weight at the box office. The obvious reputation of Shakespeare as early as 1598 makes the effort to prove him a myth one of the most absurd in the history of human perversity.

The anti-Shakespeareans talk darkly about a plot of vested interests to maintain the authorship of Shakespeare. Nobody has any vested interest in Shakespeare, but every scholar is interested in the truth and in the quality of evidence advanced by special pleaders who set forth hypotheses in place of facts.

The anti-Shakespeareans base their arguments upon a few simple premises, all of them false. These false premises are that Shakespeare was an unlettered yokel without any schooling, that nothing is known about Shakespeare, and that only a noble lord or the equivalent in background could have written the plays. The facts are that more is known about Shakespeare than about most dramatists of his day, that he had a very good education, acquired in the Stratford Grammar School, that the plays show no evidence of profound book learning, and that the knowledge of kings and courts evident in the plays is no greater than any intelligent young man could have picked up at second hand. Most anti-Shakespeareans are naïve and betray an obvious snobbery. The author of their favorite plays, they imply, must have had a college diploma framed and hung on his study wall like the one in their dentist's office, and obviously so great a writer must have had a title or some equally significant evidence of exalted social background. They forget that genius has a way of cropping up in unexpected places and that none of the great creative writers of the world got his inspiration in a college or university course.

William Shakespeare was the son of John Shakespeare of Stratford-upon-Avon, a substantial citizen of that small but busy market town in the center of the rich agricultural county of Warwick. John Shakespeare kept a shop, what we would call a general store; he dealt in wool and other produce and gradually acquired property. As a youth, John Shakespeare had learned the trade of glover and leather worker. There is no contemporary evidence that the elder Shakespeare was a butcher, though the anti-Shakespeareans like to talk about the ignorant "butcher's boy of Stratford." Their only evidence is a statement by gossipy John Aubrey, more than a century after William Shakespeare's birth, that young William followed his father's trade, and when he killed a calf, "he would do it in a high style and make a speech." We would like to believe the story true, but Aubrey is not a very credible witness.

John Shakespeare probably continued to operate a farm at Snitterfield that his father had leased. He married Mary Arden, daughter of his father's landlord, a man of some property. The third of their eight children was William, baptized on April 26, 1564, and probably born three days before. At least, it is conventional to celebrate April 23 as his birthday.

The Stratford records give considerable information about John Shakespeare. We know that he held several municipal offices including those of alderman and mayor. In 1580 he was in some sort of legal difficulty and was fined for neglecting a summons of the Court of Queen's Bench requiring him to appear at Westminster and be bound over to keep the peace.

As a citizen and alderman of Stratford, John Shakespeare was entitled to send his son to the grammar school free. Though the records are lost, there can be no reason to doubt that this is where young William received his education. As any student of the period knows, the grammar schools provided the basic education in Latin learning and literature. The Elizabethan grammar school is not to be confused with modern grammar schools. Many cultivated men of the day received all their formal education in the grammar schools. At the universities in this period a student would have received little training that would have inspired him to be a creative writer. At Stratford young Shakespeare would have acquired a familiarity with Latin and some little knowledge of Greek. He would have read Latin authors and become acquainted with the plays of Plautus and Terence. Undoubtedly, in this period of his life he received that stimulation to read and explore for himself the world of ancient and modern history which he later utilized in his plays. The youngster who does not acquire this type of intellectual curiosity *before* college days rarely develops as a result of a college course the kind of mind Shakespeare demonstrated. His learning in books was anything but profound, but he clearly had the probing curiosity that sent him in search of information, and he had a keenness in the observation of nature and of humankind that finds reflection in his poetry.

There is little documentation for Shakespeare's boyhood. There is little reason why there should be. Nobody knew that he was going to be a dramatist about whom any scrap of information would be prized in the centuries to come. He was merely an active and vigorous youth of Stratford, perhaps assisting his father in his business, and no Boswell bothered to write down facts about him. The most important record that we have is a marriage license issued by the Bishop of Worcester on November 28, 1582, to permit William Shakespeare to marry Anne Hathaway, seven or eight years his senior; furthermore, the Bishop permitted the marriage after reading the banns only once instead of three times, evidence of the desire for haste. The need was explained on May 26, 1583, when the christening of Susanna, daughter of William and Anne Shakespeare, was recorded at Stratford. Two years later, on February 2, 1585, the records show the birth of twins to the Shakespeares, a boy and a girl who were christened Hamnet and Judith.

What William Shakespeare was doing in Stratford during the early years of his married life, or when he went to London, we do not know. It has been conjectured that he tried his hand at schoolteaching, but that is a mere guess. There is a legend that he left Stratford to escape a charge of poaching in the park of Sir Thomas Lucy of Charlecote, but there is no proof of this. There is also a legend that when first he came to London, he earned his living by holding horses outside a playhouse and presently was given employment inside, but there is nothing better than eighteenth-century hearsay for this. How Shakespeare broke into the London theatres as a dramatist and actor we do not know. But lack of information is not surprising, for Elizabethans did not write their autobiographies, and we know even less about the lives of many writers and some men of affairs than we know about Shakespeare. By 1592 he was so well established and popular that he incurred the envy of the dramatist and pamphleteer Robert Greene, who referred to him as an "upstart crow . . . in his own conceit the only Shake-scene in a country." From this time onward, contemporary allusions and references in legal documents enable the scholar to chart Shakespeare's career with greater accuracy than is possible with most other Elizabethan dramatists.

By 1594 Shakespeare was a member of the company of actors known as the Lord Chamberlain's Men. After the accession of James I, in 1603, the company would have the sovereign for their patron and would be known as the King's Men. During the period of its greatest prosperity, this company would have as its principal theatres the Globe and the Blackfriars. Shakespeare was both an actor and a shareholder in the company. Tradition has assigned him such acting roles as Adam in *As You Like It* and the Ghost in *Hamlet,* a modest place on the stage that suggests that he may have had other duties in the management of the company. Such conclusions, however, are based on surmise.

What we do know is that his plays were popular and that he was highly successful in his vocation. His first play may have been *The Comedy of Errors,* acted perhaps in 1591. Certainly this was one of his earliest plays. The three parts of *Henry VI* were acted sometime between 1590 and 1592. Critics are not in agreement about precisely how much Shakespeare wrote of these three plays. *Richard III* probably dates from 1593. With this play Shakespeare captured the imagination of Elizabethan audiences, then enormously interested in historical plays. With *Richard III* Shakespeare also gave an interpretation pleasing to the Tudors of the rise to power of the grandfather of Queen Elizabeth. From this time onward, Shakespeare's plays followed on the stage in rapid succession: *Titus Andronicus, The Taming of the Shrew, The Two Gentlemen of Verona, Love's Labour's Lost, Romeo and Juliet, Richard II, A Midsummer Night's Dream, King John, The Merchant of Venice, Henry IV,* Pts. I and II, *Much Ado About Nothing, Henry V, Julius Cæsar, As You Like It, Twelfth Night, Hamlet, The Merry Wives of Windsor, All's Well That Ends Well, Measure for Measure, Othello, King Lear,* and nine others that followed before Shakespeare retired completely, about 1613.

In the course of his career in London, he made enough money to enable him to retire to Stratford with a competence. His purchase on May 4, 1597, of New Place, then the second-largest dwelling in Stratford, a "pretty house of brick and timber," with a handsome garden, indicates his increasing prosperity. There his wife and children lived while he busied himself in the London theatres. The summer before he acquired New Place, his life was darkened by the death of his only son, Hamnet, a child of eleven. In May, 1602, Shakespeare purchased one hundred and seven acres of fertile farmland near Stratford and a few months later bought a cottage and garden across the alley from New Place. About 1611, he seems to have returned permanently to Stratford, for the next year a legal document refers to him as "William Shakespeare of Stratford-upon-Avon . . . gentleman." To achieve the desired appellation of gentleman, William Shakespeare had seen to it that the College of Heralds in 1596 granted his father a coat of arms. In one step he thus became a second-generation gentleman.

Shakespeare's daughter Susanna made a good match in 1607 with Dr. John Hall, a prominent and prosperous Stratford physician. His second daughter, Judith, did not marry until she was thirty-two years old, and then, under somewhat scandalous circumstances, she married Thomas Quiney, a Stratford vintner. On March 25, 1616, Shakespeare made his will, bequeathing his landed property to Susanna, £300 to Judith, certain sums to other relatives, and his second-best bed to his wife, Anne. Much has been made of the second-best bed, but the legacy probably indicates only that Anne liked that particular bed. Shakespeare, following the practice of the time, may have already arranged with Susanna for his wife's care. Finally, on April 23, 1616, the anniversary of his birth, William Shakespeare died, and he was buried on April 25 within the chancel of Trinity Church, as befitted an honored citizen. On August 6, 1623, a few months before the publication of the collected edition of Shakespeare's plays, Anne Shakespeare joined her husband in death.

THE PUBLICATION OF HIS PLAYS

DURING HIS LIFETIME Shakespeare made no effort to publish any of his plays, though eighteen appeared in print in single-play editions known as quartos. Some of these are corrupt versions known as "bad quartos." No quarto, so far as is known, had the author's approval. Plays were not considered "literature" any more than radio and television scripts today are considered literature. Dramatists sold their plays outright to the theatrical companies and it was usually considered in the company's interest to keep plays from getting into print. To achieve a reputation as a man of letters, Shakespeare wrote his *Sonnets* and his narrative poems, *Venus and Adonis* and *The Rape of Lucrece,* but he probably never dreamed that his plays would establish his reputation as a literary genius. Only Ben Jonson, a man known for his colossal conceit, had the crust to call his plays *Works,* as he did when he published an edition in 1616 But men laughed at Ben Jonson.

After Shakespeare's death, two of his old colleagues in the King's Men, John Heming and Henry Condell, decided that it would be a good thing to print, in more accurate versions than were then available, the plays already published and eighteen additional plays not previously published in quarto. In 1623 appeared *Mr.*

William Shakespeares Comedies, Histories, & Tragedies. Published according to the True Originall Copies. London. Printed by Isaac Iaggard and Ed. Blount. This was the famous First Folio, a work that had the authority of Shakespeare's associates. The only play commonly attributed to Shakespeare that was omitted in the First Folio was *Pericles.* In their preface, "To the great Variety of Readers," Heming and Condell state that whereas "you were abused with diverse stolen and surreptitious copies, maimed and deformed by the frauds and stealths of injurious impostors that exposed them, even those are now offered to your view cured and perfect of their limbs; and all the rest, absolute in their numbers, as he conceived them." What they used for printer's copy is one of the vexed problems of scholarship, and skilled bibliographers have devoted years of study to the question of the relation of the "copy" for the First Folio to Shakespeare's manuscripts. In some cases it is clear that the editors corrected printed quarto versions of the plays, probably by comparison with playhouse scripts. Whether these scripts were in Shakespeare's autograph is anybody's guess. No manuscript of any play in Shakespeare's handwriting has survived. Indeed, very few play manuscripts from this period by any author are extant. The Tudor and Stuart periods had not yet learned to prize autographs and authors' original manuscripts.

Since the First Folio contains eighteen plays not previously printed, it is the only source for these. For the other eighteen, which had appeared in quarto versions, the First Folio also has the authority of an edition prepared and overseen by Shakespeare's colleagues and professional associates. But since editorial standards in 1623 were far from strict, and Heming and Condell were actors rather than editors by profession, the texts are sometimes careless. The printing and proofreading of the First Folio also left much to be desired, and some garbled passages have to be corrected and emended. The "good quarto" texts have to be taken into account in preparing a modern edition.

Because of the great popularity of Shakespeare through the centuries, the First Folio has become a prized book, but it is not a very rare one, for it is estimated that 238 copies are extant. The Folger Shakespeare Library in Washington, D.C., has seventy-nine copies of the First Folio, collected by the founder, Henry Clay Folger, who believed that a collation of as many texts as possible would reveal significant facts about the text of Shakespeare's plays. Dr. Charlton Hinman, using an ingenious machine of his own invention for mechanical collating, has made many discoveries that throw light on Shakespeare's text and on printing practices of the day.

The probability is that the First Folio of 1623 had an edition of between 1,000 and 1,250 copies. It is believed that it sold for £1, which made it an expensive book, for £1 in 1623 was equivalent to something between $40 and $50 in modern purchasing power.

During the seventeenth century, Shakespeare was sufficiently popular to warrant three later editions in folio size, the Second Folio of 1632, the Third Folio of 1663-1664, and the Fourth Folio of 1685. The Third Folio added six other plays ascribed to Shakespeare, but these are apocryphal.

THE THEATRES in which Shakespeare's plays were performed were vastly different from those we know today. The stage was a platform that jutted out into the area now occupied by the first rows of seats on the main floor, what is called the "orchestra" in America and the "pit" in England. This platform had no curtain to come down at the ends of acts and scenes. And although simple stage properties were available, the Elizabethan theatre lacked both the machinery and the elaborate movable scenery of the modern theatre. In the rear of the platform stage was a curtained area that could be used as an inner room, a tomb, or any such scene that might be required. A balcony above this inner room, and perhaps balconies on the sides of the stage, could represent the upper deck of a ship, the entry to Juliet's room, or a prison window. A trap door in the stage provided an entrance for ghosts and devils from the nether regions, and a similar trap in the canopied structure over the stage, known as the "heavens," made it possible to let down angels on a rope. These primitive stage arrangements help to account for many elements in Elizabethan plays. For example, since there was no curtain, the dramatist frequently felt the necessity of writing into his play action to clear the stage at the ends of acts and scenes. The funeral march at the end of *Hamlet* is not there merely for atmosphere; Shakespeare had to get the corpses off the stage. The lack of scenery also freed the dramatist from undue concern about the exact location of his sets, and the physical relation of his various settings to each other did not have to be worked out with the same precision as in the modern theatre.

Before London had buildings designed exclusively for theatrical entertainment, plays were given in inns and taverns. The characteristic inn of the period had an inner courtyard with rooms opening onto balconies overlooking the yard. Players could set up their temporary stages at one end of the yard and audiences could find seats on the balconies out of the weather. The poorer sort could stand or sit on the cobblestones in the yard, which was open to the sky. The first theatres followed this construction, and throughout the Elizabethan period the large public theatres had a yard in front of the stage open to the weather, with two or three tiers of covered balconies extending around the theatre. This physical structure again influenced the writing of plays. Because a dramatist wanted the actors to be heard, he frequently wrote into his play orations that could be delivered with declamatory effect. He also provided spectacle, buffoonery, and broad jests to keep the riotous groundlings in the yard entertained and quiet.

In another respect the Elizabethan theatre differed greatly from ours. It had no actresses. All women's roles were taken by boys, sometimes recruited from the boys' choirs of the London churches. Some of these youths acted their roles with great skill and the Elizabethans did not seem to be aware of any incongruity. The first actresses on the professional English stage appeared after the Restoration of Charles II, in 1660, when exiled Englishmen brought back from France practices of the French stage.

London in the Elizabethan period, as now, was the

center of theatrical interest, though wandering actors from time to time traveled through the country performing in inns, halls, and the houses of the nobility. The first professional playhouse, called simply The Theatre, was erected by James Burbage, father of Shakespeare's colleague Richard Burbage, in 1576 on lands of the old Holywell Priory adjacent to Finsbury Fields, a playground and park area just north of the city walls. It had the advantage of being outside the city's jurisdiction and yet was near enough to be easily accessible. Soon after The Theatre was opened, another playhouse called The Curtain was erected in the same neighborhood. Both of these playhouses had open courtyards and were probably polygonal in shape.

About the time The Curtain opened, Richard Farrant, Master of the Children of the Chapel Royal at Windsor and of St. Paul's, conceived the idea of opening a "private" theatre in the old monastery buildings of the Blackfriars, not far from St. Paul's Cathedral in the heart of the city. This theatre was ostensibly to train the choirboys in plays for presentation at Court, but Farrant managed to present plays to paying audiences and achieved considerable success until aristocratic neighbors complained and had the theatre closed. This first Blackfriars Theatre was significant, however, because it popularized the boy actors in a professional way and it paved the way for a second theatre in the Blackfriars, which Shakespeare's company took over more than thirty years later. By the last years of the sixteenth century, London had at least six professional theatres and still others were erected during the reign of James I.

The Globe Theatre, the playhouse that most people connect with Shakespeare, was erected early in 1599 on the Bankside, the area across the Thames from the city. Its construction had a dramatic beginning, for on the night of December 28, 1598, James Burbage's sons, Cuthbert and Richard, gathered together a crew who tore down the old theatre in Holywell and carted the timbers across the river to a site that they had chosen for a new playhouse. The reason for this clandestine operation was a row with the landowner over the lease to the Holywell property. The site chosen for the Globe was another playground outside of the city's jurisdiction, a region of somewhat unsavory character. Not far away was the Bear Garden, an amphitheatre devoted to the baiting of bears and bulls. This was also the region occupied by many houses of ill fame licensed by the Bishop of Winchester and the source of substantial revenue to him. But it was easily accessible either from London Bridge or by means of the cheap boats operated by the London watermen, and it had the great advantage of being beyond the authority of the Puritanical aldermen of London, who frowned on plays because they lured apprentices from work, filled their heads with improper ideas, and generally exerted a bad influence. The aldermen also complained that the crowds drawn together in the theatre helped to spread the plague.

The Globe was the handsomest theatre up to its time. It was a large building, apparently octagonal in shape and open like its predecessors to the sky in the center, but capable of seating a large audience in its covered balconies. To erect and operate the Globe, the Burbages organized a syndicate composed of the leading members of the dramatic company, of which Shakespeare was a member. Since it was open to the weather and depended on natural light, plays had to be given in the afternoon. This caused no hardship in the long afternoons of an English summer, but in the winter the weather was a great handicap and discouraged all except the hardiest. For that reason, in 1608 Shakespeare's company was glad to take over the lease of the second Blackfriars Theatre, a substantial, roomy hall reconstructed within the framework of the old monastery building. This theatre was protected from the weather and its stage was artificially lighted by chandeliers of candles. This became the winter playhouse for Shakespeare's company and at once proved so popular that the congestion of traffic created an embarrassing problem. Stringent regulations had to be made for the movement of coaches in the vicinity. Shakespeare's company continued to use the Globe during the summer months. In 1613 a squib fired from a cannon during a performance of *Henry VIII* fell on the thatched roof and the Globe burned to the ground. The next year it was rebuilt.

London had other famous theatres. The Rose, just west of the Globe, was built by Philip Henslowe, a semi-literate denizen of the Bankside, who became one of the most important theatrical owners and producers of the Tudor and Stuart periods. What is more important for historians, he kept a detailed account book, which provides much of our information about theatrical history in his time. Another famous theatre on the Bankside was the Swan, which a Dutch priest, Johannes de Witt, visited in 1596. The crude drawing of the stage which he made was copied by his friend Arend van Buchell; it is one of the important pieces of contemporary evidence for theatrical construction. Among the other theatres, the Fortune, north of the city, on Golding

Lane, and the Red Bull, even farther away from the city, off St. John's Street, were the most popular. The Red Bull, much frequented by apprentices, favored sensational and sometimes rowdy plays.

The actors who kept all of these theatres going were organized into companies under the protection of some noble patron. Traditionally actors had enjoyed a low reputation. In some of the ordinances they were classed as vagrants; in the phraseology of the time, "rogues, vagabonds, sturdy beggars, and common players" were all listed together as undesirables. To escape penalties often meted out to these characters, organized groups of actors managed to gain the protection of various personages of high degree. In the later years of Elizabeth's reign, a group flourished under the name of the Queen's Men; another group had the protection of the Lord Admiral and were known as the Lord Admiral's Men. Edward Alleyn, son-in-law of Philip Henslowe, was the leading spirit in the Lord Admiral's Men. Besides the adult companies, troupes of boy actors from time to time also enjoyed considerable popularity. Among these were the Children of Paul's and the Children of the Chapel Royal.

The company with which Shakespeare had a long association had for its first patron Henry Carey, Lord Hunsdon, the Lord Chamberlain, and hence they were known as the Lord Chamberlain's Men. After the accession of James I, they became the King's Men. This company was the great rival of the Lord Admiral's Men, managed by Henslowe and Alleyn.

All was not easy for the players in Shakespeare's time, for the aldermen of London were always eager for an excuse to close up the Blackfriars and any other theatres in their jurisdiction. The theatres outside the jurisdiction of London were not immune from interference, for they might be shut up by order of the Privy Council for meddling in politics or for various other offenses, or they might be closed in time of plague lest they spread infection. During plague times, the actors usually went on tour and played the provinces wherever they could find an audience. Particularly frightening were the plagues of 1592-1594 and 1613 when the theatres closed and the players, like many other Londoners, had to take to the country.

Though players had a low social status, they enjoyed great popularity, and one of the favorite forms of entertainment at Court was the performance of plays. To be commanded to perform at Court conferred great prestige upon a company of players, and printers frequently noted that fact when they published plays. Several of Shakespeare's plays were performed before the sovereign, and Shakespeare himself undoubtedly acted in some of these plays.

REFERENCES FOR FURTHER READING

MANY READERS will want suggestions for further reading about Shakespeare and his times. The literature in this field is enormous but a few references will serve as guides to further study. A simple and useful little book is Gerald Sanders, *A Shakespeare Primer* (New York, 1950). *A Companion to Shakespeare Studies*, edited by Harley Granville-Barker and G. B. Harrison (Cambridge, Eng., 1934) is a valuable guide. More detailed but still not too voluminous to be confusing is Hazelton Spencer, *The Art and Life of William Shakespeare* (New York, 1940) which, like Sanders' handbook, contain a brief annotated list of useful books on various aspects of the subject. The most detailed and scholarly work providing complete factual information about Shakespeare is Sir Edmund Chambers, *William Shakespeare: A Study of Facts and Problems* (2 vols., Oxford, 1930). For detailed, factual information about the Elizabethan and seventeenth-century stages, the definitive reference works are Sir Edmund Chambers, *The Elizabethan Stage* (4 vols., Oxford, 1923) and Gerald E. Bentley, *The Jacobean and Caroline Stage* (5 vols., Oxford, 1941-1956). Alfred Harbage, *Shakespeare's Audience* (New York, 1941) throws light on the nature and tastes of the customers for whom Elizabethan dramatists wrote.

Although specialists disagree about details of stage construction, the reader will find essential information in John C. Adams, *The Globe Playhouse: Its Design and Equipment* (Barnes & Noble, 1961). A model of the Globe playhouse by Dr. Adams is on permanent exhibition in the Folger Shakespeare Library in Washington, D.C. An excellent description of the architecture of the Globe is Irwin Smith, *Shakespeare's Globe Playhouse: A Modern Reconstruction in Text and Scale Drawings Based upon the Reconstruction of the Globe by John Cranford Adams* (New York, 1956). Another recent study of the physical characteristics of the Globe is C. Walter Hodges, *The Globe Restored* (London, 1953). An easily read history of the early theatres is J. Q. Adams, *Shakespearean Playhouses: A History of English Theatres from the Beginnings to the Restoration* (Boston, 1917).

The following titles on theatrical history will provide information about Shakespeare's plays in later periods:

Alfred Harbage, *Theatre for Shakespeare* (Toronto, 1955); Esther Cloudman Dunn, *Shakespeare in America* (New York, 1939); George C. D. Odell, *Shakespeare from Betterton to Irving* (2 vols., London, 1921); Arthur Colby Sprague, *Shakespeare and the Actors: The Stage Business in His Plays (1660–1905)* (Cambridge, Mass., 1944) and *Shakespearian Players and Performances* (Cambridge, Mass., 1953); Leslie A. Hotson, *The Commonwealth and Restoration Stage* (Cambridge, Mass., 1928); Alwin Thaler, *Shakspere to Sheridan: A Book About the Theatre of Yesterday and To-day* (Cambridge, Mass., 1922); Ernest Bradlee Watson, *Sheridan to Robertson: A Study of the 19th-Century London Stage* (Cambridge, Mass., 1926). Enid Welsford, *The Court Masque* (Cambridge, Eng., 1927) is an excellent study of the characteristics of this form of entertainment.

Harley Granville-Barker, *Prefaces to Shakespeare* (5 vols., London, 1927–1948) provides stimulating critical discussion of the plays. An older classic of criticism is Andrew C. Bradley, *Shakespearean Tragedy: Lectures on Hamlet, Othello, King Lear, Macbeth* (London, 1904), which is now available in an inexpensive reprint (New York, 1955). Thomas M. Parrott, *Shakespearean Comedy* (New York, 1949) is scholarly and readable. Shakespeare's dramatizations of English history are examined in E. M. W. Tillyard, *Shakespeare's History Plays* (London, 1948), and Lily Bess Campbell, *Shakespeare's "Histories," Mirrors of Elizabethan Policy* (San Marino, Calif., 1947) contains a more technical discussion of the same subject.

Interesting pictures as well as new information about Shakespeare will be found in F. E. Halliday, *Shakespeare, a Pictorial Biography* (London, 1956). Allardyce

Nicoll, *The Elizabethans* (Cambridge, Eng., 1957) contains a variety of illustrtaions for the period.

A brief, clear, and accurate account of Tudor history is S. T. Bindoff, *The Tudors,* in the Penguin series. A readable general history is G. M. Trevelyan, *The History of England,* first published in 1926 and available in many editions. G. M. Trevelyan, *English Social History,* first published in 1942 and also available in many editions, provides fascinating information about England in all periods. Sir John Neale, *Queen Elizabeth* (London, 1934) is the best study of the Great Queen. Various aspects of life in the Elizabethan period are treated in Louis B. Wright, *Middle-Class Culture in Elizabethan England* (Chapel Hill, N.C., 1935; reprinted by Cornell University Press, 1958). *Shakespeare's England: An Account of the Life and Manners of His Age,* edited by Sidney Lee and C. T. Onions (2 vols., Oxford, 1916), provides a large amount of information on many aspects of life in the Elizabethan period. Additional information will be found in Muriel St. C. Byrne, *Elizabethan Life in Town and Country* (Barnes & Noble, 1961).

The Folger Shakespeare Library is currently publishing a series of illustrated pamphlets on various aspects of English life in the sixteenth and seventeenth centuries. The following titles are available: Dorothy E. Mason, *Music in Elizabethan England;* Craig R. Thompson, *The English Church in the Sixteenth Century;* Louis B. Wright, *Shakespeare's Theatre and the Dramatic Tradition;* Giles E. Dawson, *The Life of William Shakespeare;* Virginia A. LaMar, *English Dress in the Age of Shakespeare;* Craig R. Thompson, *The Bible in English, 1525-1611;* Craig R. Thompson, *Schools in Tudor England.*

[Dramatis Personae.

Theseus, Duke of Athens.
Egeus, father to *Hermia*.
Lysander,
Demetrius, } in love with *Hermia*.

Philostrate, Master of the Revels to *Theseus*.

Peter Quince, a carpenter.
Nick Bottom, a weaver.
Francis Flute, a bellows-mender.
Tom Snout, a tinker.
Snug, a joiner.
Robin Starveling, a tailor.

Hippolyta, Queen of the Amazons, betrothed to
  Theseus.
Hermia, daughter to *Egeus*, in love with
  Lysander.
Helena, in love with *Demetrius*.

Oberon, King of the Fairies.
Titania, Queen of the Fairies.
Puck, or *Robin Goodfellow*.
Peaseblossom,
Cobweb,
Moth, } fairies.
Mustardseed,

Other fairies attending *Oberon* and *Titania;* attendants on *Theseus* and *Hippolyta*.

SCENE: *Athens, and a wood near it.*]

A
MIDSUMMER
NIGHT'S
DREAM

ACT I

I. [i.] Theseus, Duke of Athens, and his bride-to-be, Hippolyta, Queen of the Amazons, are planning the festivities for their forthcoming wedding when Egeus enters with his daughter, Hermia, and her two suitors, Lysander and Demetrius. Egeus complains that Hermia prefers Lysander and refuses to marry his own choice, Demetrius, and requests that the Athenian law be enforced if she persists in her disobedience. Theseus agrees that Hermia must either marry Demetrius, take a vow of eternal chastity, or be put to death. Hermia and Lysander secretly plan to meet in a wood outside of Athens with the intention of fleeing to take refuge with Lysander's aunt, outside the jurisdiction of Athens. Helena, Hermia's closest friend, whom Demetrius had wooed before he met Hermia, is told of their plan and decides to reveal it to Demetrius, whom she still loves.

<hr />

5. **dowager:** a widow with a life interest in her husband's estate.

7. **steep:** soak.

10. **New-bent:** Nicholas Rowe's emendation for "now bent" in the First Quarto and First Folio.

14. **pert:** sprightly.

16. **companion:** fellow, in a derogatory sense.

17. **Hippolyta, I wooed thee with my sword:** a reference to Theseus' capture of Hippolyta in his war with the Amazons.

20. **triumph:** pageantry.

1

ACT I

iiiiiiiiiiiiiiiiiiiiiiiiiiiiiiiiiiiiiiiiiiiiiiiiiiiiiiiiiiiiiiiiiiiiiiiiiiiiiiiiiiiiiiiiiiiiiiiiiiiiiiiiiiiiiiii

[Scene I. Athens. The Palace of Theseus.]

Enter *Theseus, Hippolyta,* [*Philostrate,*] with others.

The. Now, fair Hippolyta, our nuptial hour
Draws on apace; four happy days bring in
Another moon: but, O, methinks, how slow
This old moon wanes! she lingers my desires,
Like to a stepdame or a dowager,   5
Long withering out a young man's revenue.
   Hip. Four days will quickly steep themselves in night;
Four nights will quickly dream away the time;
And then the moon, like to a silver bow
New-bent in heaven, shall behold the night   10
Of our solemnities.
   The.   Go, Philostrate,
Stir up the Athenian youth to merriments,
Awake the pert and nimble spirit of mirth,
Turn melancholy forth to funerals;   15
The pale companion is not for our pomp.
                       [*Exit Philostrate.*]
Hippolyta, I wooed thee with my sword,
And won thy love doing thee injuries;
But I will wed thee in another key,
With pomp, with triumph, and with revelling.   20

The Battle with the Amazons.
From Ovid, *Metamorphoses* (1509).

33. **stol'n the impression of her fantasy:** slyly made himself an object of love in her imagination.

34. **gauds:** cheap trinkets; **conceits:** ingeniously contrived gifts.

35. **Knacks:** knickknacks, trifles.

36. **unhardened:** inexperienced and therefore malleable.

40. **Be it so:** if it be so.

46. **Immediately:** expressly.

47. **Be advised:** consider your position carefully.

Enter *Egeus* and his daughter *Hermia*, *Lysander*, and
Demetrius.

Ege. Happy be Theseus, our renowned duke!
The. Thanks, good Egeus: what's the news with thee?
Ege. Full of vexation come I, with complaint
Against my child, my daughter Hermia.
Stand forth, Demetrius. My noble lord,   25
This man hath my consent to marry her.
Stand forth, Lysander. And, my gracious duke,
This man hath bewitched the bosom of my child.
Thou, thou, Lysander, thou hast given her rhymes
And interchanged love tokens with my child;   30
Thou hast by moonlight at her window sung
With feigning voice verses of feigning love,
And stol'n the impression of her fantasy
With bracelets of thy hair, rings, gauds, conceits,
Knacks, trifles, nosegays, sweetmeats—messengers   35
Of strong prevailment in unhardened youth.
With cunning hast thou filched my daughter's heart,
Turned her obedience, which is due to me,
To stubborn harshness. And, my gracious duke,
Be it so she will not here before your Grace   40
Consent to marry with Demetrius,
I beg the ancient privilege of Athens,
As she is mine, I may dispose of her,
Which shall be either to this gentleman
Or to her death, according to our law   45
Immediately provided in that case.
The. What say you, Hermia? Be advised, fair maid,
To you your father should be as a god;

56. **kind**: respect; that is, as a husband; **wanting**: lacking; **voice**: approval.

62. **concern**: involve in a compromising way.

70. **blood**: passions.

72. **livery of a nun**: a nun's habit. This reference is not as anachronistic as it may seem at first, since Vestal Virgins of the goddess Diana led chaste lives devoted to religious observance. See ll. 91-2 below.

73. **mewed**: confined. A "mew" was a house for falcons.

75. **faint**: spiritless.

77. **pilgrimage**: course of life on earth.

78. **earthlier happy**: happier by earthly standards; **the rose distilled**: that is, to make a perfume. The life of the rose is ended more quickly by being picked, but at least it produces a perfume which lives after it for a time.

One that composed your beauties; yea, and one
To whom you are but as a form in wax   50
By him imprinted and within his power
To leave the figure or disfigure it.
Demetrius is a worthy gentleman.
  Her. So is Lysander.
  The.   In himself he is;   55
But in this kind, wanting your father's voice,
The other must be held the worthier.
  Her. I would my father looked but with my eyes.
  The. Rather your eyes must with his judgment look.
  Her. I do entreat your Grace to pardon me.   60
I know not by what power I am made bold,
Nor how it may concern my modesty
In such a presence here to plead my thoughts;
But I beseech your Grace that I may know
The worst that may befall me in this case   65
If I refuse to wed Demetrius.
  The. Either to die the death, or to abjure
For ever the society of men.
Therefore, fair Hermia, question your desires,
Know of your youth, examine well your blood,   70
Whether, if you yield not to your father's choice,
You can endure the livery of a nun,
For aye to be in shady cloister mewed,
To live a barren sister all your life,
Chanting faint hymns to the cold fruitless moon.   75
Thrice blessed they that master so their blood
To undergo such maiden pilgrimage;
But earthlier happy is the rose distilled
Than that which, withering on the virgin thorn,
Grows, lives, and dies in single blessedness.   80

Vestal Virgins at their shrine.
From Cartari, *Imagini delli Dei de gl'Antichi* (1609).

82. **virgin patent:** freedom to live as a virgin.

83. **Unto his lordship:** to the mastery of that man.

90. **he would:** that is, as her father insisted.

91. **protest:** vow.

94. **crazed:** flawed, imperfect because illegal.

100. **estate unto:** bestow upon.

101. **derived:** born.

102. **possessed:** endowed with wealth.

104. **vantage:** advantage; Lysander considers that he may even exceed Demetrius in eligibility.

108. **avouch it to his head:** maintain it to his face.

112. **spotted:** impure, because faithless.

4

Her. So will I grow, so live, so die, my lord,
Ere I will yield my virgin patent up
Unto his lordship whose unwished yoke
My soul consents not to give sovereignty.
The. Take time to pause; and by the next new moon—   85
The sealing day betwixt my love and me
For everlasting bond of fellowship—
Upon that day either prepare to die
For disobedience to your father's will,
Or else to wed Demetrius, as he would,   90
Or on Diana's altar to protest
For aye austerity and single life.
Dem. Relent, sweet Hermia; and, Lysander, yield
Thy crazed title to my certain right.
Lys. You have her father's love, Demetrius;   95
Let me have Hermia's: do you marry him.
Ege. Scornful Lysander! true, he hath my love;
And what is mine my love shall render him;
And she is mine, and all my right of her
I do estate unto Demetrius.   100
Lys. I am, my lord, as well derived as he,
As well possessed; my love is more than his;
My fortunes every way as fairly ranked
(If not with vantage) as Demetrius';
And (which is more than all these boasts can be)   105
I am beloved of beauteous Hermia.
Why should not I then prosecute my right?
Demetrius, I'll avouch it to his head,
Made love to Nedar's daughter, Helena,
And won her soul; and she (sweet lady) dotes,   110
Devoutly dotes, dotes in idolatry,
Upon this spotted and inconstant man.

Theseus and Hippolyta.
From *Promptuarii Iconum* . . . (1553).

122. **extenuate**: mitigate, render less severe, referring to the Athenian law.

127. **Against**: in preparation for.

128. **nearly that concerns**: i.e., that nearly concerns; is important to.

129. **duty and desire**: eager obedience.

131. **How chance**: how does it happen that.

132. **Belike**: most likely.

133. **Beteem**: permit, allow.

134. **for aught that I could ever read**: that is, nothing I have ever read offered contrary evidence.

137. **different in blood**: unequal in birth, as Hermia's reply makes clear.

138. **cross**: misfortune; **low**: Lewis Theobald's emendation for "loue" in the First Quarto and First Folio.

139. **misgraffed**: mismated.

141. **stood**: depended.

The. I must confess that I have heard so much,
And with Demetrius thought to have spoke thereof;
But, being over-full of self-affairs,   115
My mind did lose it. But, Demetrius, come;
And come, Egeus. You shall go with me;
I have some private schooling for you both.
For you, fair Hermia, look you arm yourself
To fit your fancies to your father's will;   120
Or else the law of Athens yields you up
(Which by no means we may extenuate)
To death or to a vow of single life.
Come, my Hippolyta. What cheer, my love?
Demetrius and Egeus, go along.   125
I must employ you in some business
Against our nuptial and confer with you
Of something nearly that concerns yourselves.
    Ege. With duty and desire we follow you.
              Exeunt. Manent Lysander and Hermia.
    Lys. How now, my love? Why is your cheek so pale? 130
How chance the roses there do fade so fast?
    Her. Belike for want of rain, which I could well
Beteem them from the tempest of my eyes.
    Lys. Ay me! for aught that I could ever read,
Could ever hear by tale or history,   135
The course of true love never did run smooth;
But, either it was different in blood—
    Her. O cross! too high to be enthralled to low!
    Lys. Or else misgraffed in respect of years—
    Her. O spite! too old to be engaged to young!   140
    Lys. Or else it stood upon the choice of friends—
    Her. O hell! to choose love by another's eyes!

143. **if there were a sympathy in choice**: if the couple were suitably and harmoniously matched.

145. **momentany**: transitory. This synonym for "momentary" derives from the Latin word *momentaneus,* while "momentary" derives from *momentarius.*

147. **collied**: black, as though darkened by coal.

148. **in a spleen**: impetuously, as in a quick flash of anger. The spleen was considered the seat of hasty temper and impulsive behavior; **unfolds**: reveals.

152. **ever**: always; **crossed**: opposed, frustrated.

156. **thoughts**: anxieties, cares.

157. **Fancy's**: Love's.

158. **A good persuasion**: that is, a sound attitude for us to take.

162. **respects**: looks upon, regards.

169. **do observance to a morn of May**: take part in May Day rites.

170. **stay**: wait.

173. **his best arrow, with the golden head**: according to Ovid's *Metamorphoses,* Book I, the golden-headed arrow was used by Cupid to inspire love and an arrow with a leaden head was used to kill it.

VENUS.

Venus in her chariot and the blind Cupid.
From John Indagine, *The Book of Palmestry* (1666).

Lys. Or, if there were a sympathy in choice,
War, death, or sickness did lay siege to it,
Making it momentany as a sound,   145
Swift as a shadow, short as any dream,
Brief as the lightning in the collied night,
That, in a spleen, unfolds both heaven and earth,
And ere a man hath power to say "Behold!"
The jaws of darkness do devour it up: 150
So quick bright things come to confusion.
   Her. If then true lovers have been ever crossed,
It stands as an edict in destiny.
Then let us teach our trial patience,
Because it is a customary cross,   155
As due to love as thoughts and dreams and sighs,
Wishes and tears, poor Fancy's followers.
   Lys. A good persuasion. Therefore hear me, Hermia.
I have a widow aunt, a dowager,
Of great revenue, and she hath no child: 160
From Athens is her house remote seven leagues;
And she respects me as her only son.
There, gentle Hermia, may I marry thee;
And to that place the sharp Athenian law
Cannot pursue us. If thou lovest me then,   165
Steal forth thy father's house tomorrow night;
And in the wood, a league without the town,
Where I did meet thee once with Helena
To do observance to a morn of May,
There will I stay for thee.   170
   Her.   My good Lysander!
I swear to thee by Cupid's strongest bow,
By his best arrow, with the golden head,

174. **the simplicity of Venus' doves:** doves are proverbially gentle and harmless. In mythology they were sacred to Venus, and **Venus' doves** are an appropriate symbol for a lover to swear by.

176. **the Carthage queen:** Dido, who killed herself on a funeral pyre when deserted by Æneas, the **false Troyan** of the next line (see Virgil's *Æneid*, Book IV).

183. **speed:** prosper.

185. **your fair:** your type of beauty. Helena puns on the word "fair" (meaning "blond" and "beautiful"). She herself is blond while Hermia is dark, but Hermia's beauty is preferred by Demetrius.

186. **lodestars:** pole stars, by which travelers are guided.

187. **tuneable:** melodious.

189. **favor:** personal characteristics which attract or repel.

190. **Yours would I catch:** Thomas Hanmer's emendation for "Your words I catch" in the First Quarto and First Folio.

193. **bated:** excepted.

194. **translated:** transformed. That is, if I had all the world but lacked Demetrius, I would give all to you to be transformed to his liking.

By the simplicity of Venus' doves,
By that which knitteth souls and prospers loves,   175
And by that fire which burned the Carthage queen
When the false Troyan under sail was seen,
By all the vows that ever men have broke
(In number more than ever women spoke),
In that same place thou hast appointed me   180
Tomorrow truly will I meet with thee.
    Lys. Keep promise, love. Look, here comes Helena.

Enter *Helena.*

    Her. God speed fair Helena! Whither away?
    Hel. Call you me fair? That fair again unsay.
Demetrius loves your fair. O happy fair!   185
Your eyes are lodestars, and your tongue's sweet air
More tuneable than lark to shepherd's ear
When wheat is green, when hawthorn buds appear.
Sickness is catching. O, were favor so,
Yours would I catch, fair Hermia, ere I go!   190
My ear should catch your voice, my eye your eye,
My tongue should catch your tongue's sweet melody.
Were the world mine, Demetrius being bated,
The rest I'd give to be to you translated.
O, teach me how you look, and with what art   195
You sway the motion of Demetrius' heart!
    Her. I frown upon him, yet he loves me still.
    Hel. O that your frowns would teach my smiles such
      skill!
    Her. I give him curses, yet he gives me love.   200
    Hel. O that my prayers could such affection move!
    Her. The more I hate, the more he follows me.

212. **he hath turned a heaven unto a hell**: that is, she was divinely happy before she loved Lysander and found her love frustrated.

214. **Phœbe**: Diana, the moon goddess.

217. **still**: always.

218. **Athens**: used as an adjective.

220. **faint**: pale.

221. **sweet**: Theobald's emendation for "sweld" in the First Quarto and First Folio.

224. **stranger companies**: Theobald's emendation for "strange companions" in the First Quarto and First Folio.

232. **How happy some o'er other some can be**: how much happier some can be than others.

Hel. The more I love, the more he hateth me.

Her. His folly, Helena, is no fault of mine.

Hel. None but your beauty: would that fault were 205
   mine!

Her. Take comfort, he no more shall see my face;
Lysander and myself will fly this place.
Before the time I did Lysander see,
Seemed Athens as a paradise to me.   210
O, then, what graces in my love do dwell
That he hath turned a heaven unto a hell!

Lys. Helen, to you our minds we will unfold:
Tomorrow night, when Phœbe doth behold
Her silver visage in the wat'ry glass,   215
Decking with liquid pearl the bladed grass
(A time that lovers' flights doth still conceal),
Through Athens gates have we devised to steal.

Her. And in the wood where often you and I
Upon faint primrose beds were wont to lie,   220
Emptying our bosoms of their counsel sweet,
There my Lysander and myself shall meet,
And thence from Athens turn away our eyes
To seek new friends and stranger companies.
Farewell, sweet playfellow. Pray thou for us;   225
And good luck grant thee thy Demetrius!
Keep word, Lysander. We must starve our sight
From lovers' food till morrow deep midnight.

Lys. I will, my Hermia.

                            Exit Hermia.

               Helena, adieu.   230
As you on him, Demetrius dote on you!   *Exit.*

Hel. How happy some o'er other some can be!
Through Athens I am thought as fair as she.

237. **So I:** so I err.

238. **quantity:** value.

242. **of any judgment taste:** any touch of judgment.

243. **figure:** portray; **unheedy haste:** that is, the wings permit speed toward objectives which the eyes cannot see.

246. **waggish:** playful; **game:** fun.

248. **eyne:** eyes; an old-fashioned form used for rhyme here.

254. **intelligence:** information.

255. **If I have thanks, it is a dear expense:** that is, in view of Demetrius' present aversion to her, she will be lucky if he as much as thanks her.

The blind Cupid and his victims.
From Cartari, *Imagini delli Dei de gl'Antichi* (1615).

But what of that? Demetrius thinks not so;
He will not know what all but he do know.   235
And as he errs, doting on Hermia's eyes,
So I, admiring of his qualities.
Things base and vile, holding no quantity,
Love can transpose to form and dignity.
Love looks not with the eyes, but with the mind;   240
And therefore is winged Cupid painted blind.
Nor hath Love's mind of any judgment taste:
Wings, and no eyes, figure unheedy haste.
And therefore is Love said to be a child,
Because in choice he is so oft beguiled.   245
As waggish boys in game themselves forswear,
So the boy Love is perjured everywhere;
For ere Demetrius looked on Hermia's eyne,
He hailed down oaths that he was only mine;
And when this hail some heat from Hermia felt,   250
So he dissolved, and show'rs of oaths did melt.
I will go tell him of fair Hermia's flight.
Then to the wood will he tomorrow night
Pursue her; and for this intelligence
If I have thanks, it is a dear expense;   255
But herein mean I to enrich my pain,
To have his sight thither and back again.

                                              Exit.

I. [ii.] A company of artisans plan an interlude as part of the entertainment for Theseus' wedding. "The most Lamentable Comedy and most Cruel Death of Pyramus and Thisby" is chosen and the part of Pyramus assigned to Nick Bottom, the weaver; Thisby to Francis Flute, the bellows-mender. When everyone is satisfied with his part, all agree to meet in a wood outside of the city to rehearse.

⁙⁙⁙⁙⁙⁙⁙⁙⁙⁙⁙

Entrance, l. 1. **Joiner:** that is, cabinetmaker.
Entrance, l. 2. **Tinker:** a mender of pots and pans.
2. **You were best:** it would be best for you; **generally:** Bottom's mistake for "severally." The comic dialogue of rustics conventionally contained linguistic errors and malapropisms.
3. **scrip:** script.
4. **which:** who.
9. **on:** of.
11. **Marry:** a contraction of "By the Virgin Mary," used lightly as an exclamation.
12. **Pyramus and Thisby:** Shakespeare's chief source for this "Lamentable Comedy" was probably Ovid's *Metamorphoses*, Book IV, in Arthur Golding's translation.
21. **ask:** demand.
23. **condole:** lament; **To the rest:** that is, go on with the list.

[Scene II. Athens. Quince's house.]

Enter *Quince* the Carpenter, *Snug* the Joiner, *Bottom* the Weaver, *Flute* the Bellows-mender, *Snout* the Tinker, and *Starveling* the Tailor.

Quince. Is all our company here?

Bot. You were best to call them generally, man by man, according to the scrip.

Quince. Here is the scroll of every man's name which is thought fit, through all Athens, to play in our interlude be- 5
fore the duke and the duchess on his wedding day at night.

Bot. First, good Peter Quince, say what the play treats on, then read the names of the actors, and so grow to a point. 10

Quince. Marry, our play is "The most Lamentable Comedy and most Cruel Death of Pyramus and Thisby."

Bot. A very good piece of work, I assure you, and a merry. Now, good Peter Quince, call forth your actors by the scroll. Masters, spread yourselves. 15

Quince. Answer as I call you. Nick Bottom the weaver.

Bot. Ready. Name what part I am for, and proceed.

Quince. You, Nick Bottom, are set down for Pyramus.

Bot. What is Pyramus? a lover, or a tyrant?

Quince. A lover that kills himself most gallant for love. 20

Bot. That will ask some tears in the true performing of it. If I do it, let the audience look to their eyes! I will move storms; I will condole in some measure. To the rest—

24. **a tyrant**: a character conventionally given to melodramatic ranting and violence, derived from the medieval miracle plays; **Ercles**: Hercules, the hero of classical mythology. His dialogue in Seneca's *Hercules Furens* may have established the theatrical convention of Hercules as a blustering tyrant.

25. **to tear a cat in**: that is, giving full scope for violent gestures.

30. **Phibbus**: Phoebus, the sun god.

35. **condoling**: pathetic.

43. **all one**: no matter.

44. **small**: daintily.

45. **An**: if.

46. **Thisne**: probably Bottom's pronunciation of "Thisby" in "a monstrous little voice."

Yet my chief humor is for a tyrant. I could play Ercles
rarely, or a part to tear a cat in, to make all split.   25

> "The raging rocks
> And shivering shocks
> Shall break the locks
> Of prison gates;
> And Phibbus' car   30
> Shall shine from far
> And make and mar
> The foolish Fates."

This was lofty! Now name the rest of the players. This is
Ercles' vein, a tyrant's vein. A lover is more condoling.   35
Quince. Francis Flute the bellows-mender.
Flute. Here, Peter Quince.
Quince. Flute, you must take Thisby on you.
Flute. What is Thisby? a wand'ring knight?
Quince. It is the lady that Pyramus must love.   40
Flute. Nay, faith, let not me play a woman; I have a
beard coming.
Quince. That's all one: you shall play it in a mask, and
you may speak as small as you will.
Bot. An I may hide my face, let me play Thisby too.   45
I'll speak in a monstrous little voice:—"Thisne, Thisne!"
"Ah, Pyramus, my lover dear! thy Thisby dear, and lady
dear!"
Quince. No, no! you must play Pyramus; and, Flute,
you Thisby.   50
Bot. Well, proceed.
Quince. Robin Starveling the tailor.
Starv. Here, Peter Quince.

CLOINNAMORAMENTO ET LAMORTE
DI PIRAMO ET TISBE

"The Tragedy of Pyramus and Thisby."
From a sixteenth-century Italian version of the story.

64. **that:** so that.
70. **were:** would be.
74. **aggravate:** Bottom's mistake for "decrease."
76. **an 'twere:** as if it were.
78. **a proper man as:** as admirable a man as.

12

Quince. Robin Starveling, you must play Thisby's
mother. Tom Snout the tinker.   55

Snout. Here, Peter Quince.

Quince. You, Pyramus' father; myself, Thisby's father;
Snug the joiner, you the lion's part. And I hope here is a
play fitted.

Snug. Have you the lion's part written? Pray you, if it   60
be, give it me, for I am slow of study.

Quince. You may do it extempore, for it is nothing but
roaring.

Bot. Let me play the lion too: I will roar that I will do
any man's heart good to hear me; I will roar that I will   65
make the duke say, "Let him roar again, let him roar
again."

Quince. An you should do it too terribly, you would
fright the duchess and the ladies, that they would shriek;
and that were enough to hang us all.   70

All. That would hang us, every mother's son.

Bot. I grant you, friends, if you should fright the ladies
out of their wits, they would have no more discretion but
to hang us; but I will aggravate my voice so that I will
roar you as gently as any sucking dove; I will roar you   75
an 'twere any nightingale.

Quince. You can play no part but Pyramus; for Pyramus is a sweet-faced man; a proper man as one shall see
in a summer's day; a most lovely gentlemanlike man:
therefore you must needs play Pyramus.   80

Bot. Well, I will undertake it. What beard were I best
to play it in?

Quince. Why, what you will.

Bot. I will discharge it in either your straw-color beard,

85. **purple-in-grain**: a permanent purple.

86. **French-crown-color**: that is, golden, as **perfect yellow** indicates.

87. **French crowns**: a reference to the alleged frequency of hair loss in France from venereal disease.

97. **obscenely**: a malapropism for comic effect. Bottom perhaps thinks "obscenely" means "off the scene."

100. **Hold, or cut bowstrings**: this is generally thought to be a proverbial phrase derived from archery. The meaning is: meet at the appointed time or you will be ruled out of our company as faithless.

your orange-tawny beard, your purple-in-grain beard, or   85
your French-crown-color beard, your perfect yellow.

Quince. Some of your French crowns have no hair at
all, and then you will play barefaced. But, masters, here
are your parts; and I am to entreat you, request you, and
desire you, to con them by tomorrow night; and meet me   90
in the palace wood, a mile without the town, by moonlight. There will we rehearse; for if we meet in the city,
we shall be dogged with company, and our devices
known. In the meantime I will draw a bill of properties,
such as our play wants. I pray you, fail me not.   95

Bot. We will meet; and there we may rehearse most
obscenely and courageously. Take pains; be perfect.
Adieu.

Quince. At the duke's oak we meet.

Bot. Enough. Hold, or cut bowstrings.   100

Exeunt.

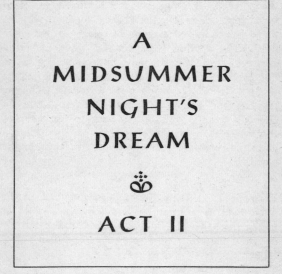

A
MIDSUMMER
NIGHT'S
DREAM

ACT II

II. [i.] The Puck (Robin Goodfellow) reveals that his master, Oberon, King of Fairies, and his Queen, Titania, have quarreled over an Indian boy, whom both wish to have in their retinues. Oberon and Titania enter and quarrel anew over the issue, and Oberon orders Puck to procure a flower which has the power of creating love for the first object seen by anyone whose eyes have been anointed with its juice. With this stratagem he plans to humiliate Titania by causing a passion for some unworthy creature; Titania thus may be compelled to relinquish the boy. Demetrius comes searching for the runaway lovers. He is pursued by Helena, whom he repulses and finally abandons. Oberon, witnessing Helena's unhappiness, orders Puck to use some of the magic juice on the eyes of a man in Athenian garments, unaware that there are two such in the wood.

꟰꟰꟰꟰꟰꟰꟰꟰꟰꟰꟰꟰꟰꟰꟰꟰꟰꟰꟰

Entrance 1. 1. **Robin Goodfellow**: the Puck of the play. Puck is a term for a mischievous sprite or goblin from the Old English *pouke*. English folklore contains many tales of the exploits of Robin Goodfellow.

3. **Thorough**: through.

4. **pale**: enclosed land, like a park.

7. **moonës**: the Middle English genitive form, used here for the sake of the meter.

ACT II

[Scene I. A wood near Athens.]

Enter a *Fairy* at one door, and [*Puck,*] *Robin Goodfellow* at another.

Puck.

Designed by Paul Konewka, a nineteenth-century German artist.

Puck. How now, spirit! whither wander you?
Fai. Over hill, over dale,
    Thorough bush, thorough brier,
    Over park, over pale,
    Thorough flood, thorough fire;
    I do wander everywhere,
    Swifter than the moonës sphere;

5

9. **orbs**: rings in the grass produced by fairy dancers.

10. **pensioners**: a reference to Queen Elizabeth's bodyguard known as Gentlemen Pensioners, who were chosen for their tall and handsome appearance.

11. **spots**: the cowslip is yellow with red spots at the center.

13. **savors**: perfume.

16. **lob**: lout.

20. **is passing fell and wrath**: is in an exceedingly fierce rage.

21. **Because that**: because.

23. **changeling**: the name usually applied to an imp left by a fairy in exchange for a human child.

25. **trace**: track, possibly in the sense of "police," or "patrol."

26. **perforce**: of necessity, forcibly.

30. **square**: quarrel; **that**: so that.

33. **shrewd**: malicious.

36. **quern**: hand mill.

37. **bootless**: uselessly (because Robin prevents the butter from turning).

38. **barm**: yeast; that is, he prevents the ale from brewing properly.

And I serve the fairy queen,
To dew her orbs upon the green.
The cowslips tall her pensioners be;   10
In their gold coats spots you see.
Those be rubies, fairy favors;
In those freckles live their savors.
I must go seek some dewdrops here,
And hang a pearl in every cowslip's ear.   15
Farewell, thou lob of spirits; I'll be gone.
Our Queen and all her elves come here anon.

Puck. The king doth keep his revels here tonight;
Take heed the queen come not within his sight:
For Oberon is passing fell and wrath,   20
Because that she, as her attendant, hath
A lovely boy, stolen from an Indian king—
She never had so sweet a changeling—
And jealous Oberon would have the child
Knight of his train, to trace the forests wild;   25
But she perforce withholds the loved boy,
Crowns him with flowers, and makes him all her joy.
And now they never meet in grove or green,
By fountain clear or spangled starlight sheen,
But they do square, that all their elves, for fear, 30
Creep into acorn cups and hide them there.

Fai. Either I mistake your shape and making quite,
Or else you are that shrewd and knavish sprite
Called Robin Goodfellow. Are not you he
That frights the maidens of the villagery;   35
Skim milk, and sometimes labor in the quern,
And bootless make the breathless housewife churn;
And sometime make the drink to bear no barm;
Mislead night-wanderers, laughing at their harm?

48. **gossip's bowl**: **gossip** was originally "godsib," i.e., godparent, but it later came to mean an elderly person fond of society and small talk. The **bowl** is a hot punch.

49. **very**: exact; **crab**: crab apple, often floated in hot, spiced drinks.

52. **aunt**: old woman; **saddest**: gravest.

54. **bum**: rump.

55. **"tailor"**: an exclamation of doubtful meaning.

56. **quire**: company; **loffe**: laugh.

57. **waxen**: increase; **neeze**: sneeze.

58. **wasted**: spent.

59. **room**: make way.

62. **Fairies**: Theobald's emendation for "fairy" in the early texts.

64. **wanton**: Oberon calls Titania an undisciplined creature because she stubbornly refuses to do as he wishes.

65. **Then I must be thy lady**: that is, "if you are to be my lord, I must be the only woman in your life."

67. **Corin**: Phillida and Corin were traditional names for lovers in pastoral verse.

Those that Hobgoblin call you, and sweet Puck,   40
You do their work, and they shall have good luck.
Are not you he?
   Puck.   Thou speakest aright;
I am that merry wanderer of the night.
I jest to Oberon, and make him smile   45
When I a fat and bean-fed horse beguile,
Neighing in likeness of a filly foal;
And sometime lurk I in a gossip's bowl
In very likeness of a roasted crab,
And when she drinks, against her lips I bob   50
And on her withered dewlap pour the ale.
The wisest aunt, telling the saddest tale,
Sometime for three-foot stool mistaketh me;
Then slip I from her bum, down topples she,
And "tailor" cries, and falls into a cough;   55
And then the whole quire hold their hips and loffe,
And waxen in their mirth, and neeze, and swear
A merrier hour was never wasted there.
But room, fairy! Here comes Oberon.
   Fai. And here my mistress. Would that he were gone! 60

Enter [Oberon] the King of Fairies, at one door, with his
   Train; and the Queen, [Titania,] at another, with hers.

   Ob. Ill met by moonlight, proud Titania.
   Queen. What, jealous Oberon! Fairies, skip hence.
I have forsworn his bed and company.
   Ob. Tarry, rash wanton: am not I thy lord?
   Queen. Then I must be thy lady; but I know   65
When thou hast stolen away from fairyland,
And in the shape of Corin sat all day,

68. **versing love:** expressing his love in poetry.

70. **steppe:** extensive plain.

71. **forsooth:** truly.

72. **buskined:** a buskin was a high shoe with elevated sole, worn by actors in Greek tragedy. Titania refers to Hippolyta's commanding height, which makes her an absurd object of a fairy's love.

76. **Glance at my credit with:** sully my reputation by means of.

79. **Perigouna:** Perigune, daughter of a murderous brigand whom Theseus killed.

80, 81. **Ægles, Ariadne, Antiopa:** North's translation of Plutarch's life of Theseus refers to these amorous conquests. **Ægles** should be "Ægle," but North spells it as Shakespeare has it here. **Ariadne,** the daughter of King Minos, fell in love with Theseus and helped him find his way out of the labyrinth and kill the Minotaur. **Antiopa,** more correctly "Antiope," was an Amazon and conflicting statements by early writers make it appear likely that "Hippolyta" and "Antiope" were the same woman.

Playing on pipes of corn, and versing love
To amorous Phillida. Why art thou here,
Come from the farthest stéppe of India,   70
But that, forsooth, the bouncing Amazon,
Your buskined mistress and your warrior love,
To Theseus must be wedded, and you come
To give their bed joy and prosperity?

    Ob. How canst thou thus, for shame, Titania,   75
Glance at my credit with Hippolyta,
Knowing I know thy love to Theseus?
Didst thou not lead him through the glimmering night
From Perigouna, whom he ravished?
And make him with fair Ægles break his faith,   80
With Ariadne, and Antiopa?

Puck and the Fairy.
Designed by Paul Konewka.

82. **forgeries:** falsehoods, fabrications.

83. **the middle summer's spring:** the midsummer's beginning.

84. **mead:** meadow.

86. **margent:** margin.

87. **ringlets:** circles, rings.

92. **pelting:** paltry, insignificant.

93. **continents:** containers.

94. **stretched his yoke:** pulled the plough.

96. **his:** its, referring to the corn.

98. **murrion:** dead of the murrain, a cattle disease.

99. **The nine men's morris:** the pattern for a game of this name, similar to checkers. Such patterns were drawn on the ground for outdoor play.

100. **quaint:** ingenious.

102. **want:** lack.

104. **governess of floods:** the moon, called by Shakespeare in *Hamlet* "the moist star," was believed to draw water as well as control the tides.

107. **thorough:** through; as a result of; **distemperature:** the unsettled order of nature.

110. **Hiems':** winter's; a personification from the Latin *hiemalis;* **thin:** a suggestion by Thomas Tyrwhitt for "chinne" in the early texts.

Queen. These are the forgeries of jealousy;
And never, since the middle summer's spring,
Met we on hill, in dale, forest, or mead,
By paved fountain or by rushy brook,   85
Or in the beached margent of the sea,
To dance our ringlets to the whistling wind,
But with thy brawls thou hast disturbed our sport.
Therefore the winds, piping to us in vain,
As in revenge, have sucked up from the sea   90
Contagious fogs; which falling in the land
Hath every pelting river made so proud
That they have overborne their continents.
The ox hath therefore stretched his yoke in vain,
The ploughman lost his sweat, and the green corn   95
Hath rotted ere his youth attained a beard;
The fold stands empty in the drowned field,
And crows are fatted with the murrion flock;
The nine men's morris is filled up with mud,
And the quaint mazes in the wanton green   100
For lack of tread are undistinguishable.
The human mortals want their winter here.
No night is now with hymn or carol blest;
Therefore the moon, the governess of floods,
Pale in her anger, washes all the air,   105
That rheumatic diseases do abound.
And thorough this distemperature we see
The seasons alter. Hoary-headed frosts
Fall in the fresh lap of the crimson rose;
And on old Hiems' thin and icy crown   110
An odorous chaplet of sweet summer buds
Is, as in mockery, set. The spring, the summer,

113. **childing**: fruitful.

114. **wonted liveries**: customary attire; **mazed**: bewildered.

115. **increase**: i.e., what they bring forth, frosts or flowers.

122. **henchman**: page, from the Middle English *henche-man*.

124. **The fairyland**: that is, the whole of fairyland.

125. **vot'ress**: devoted worshiper.

127. **Full**: an intensive; very.

128. **Neptune's**: the ocean's; Neptune was the ancient god of the sea.

129. **Marking**: taking note of.

144. **spare**: avoid.

The childing autumn, angry winter change
Their wonted liveries, and the mazed world,
By their increase, now knows not which is which.   115
And this same progeny of evils comes
From our debate, from our dissension;
We are their parents and original.

    Ob. Do you amend it then; it lies in you.
Why should Titania cross her Oberon?   120
I do but beg a little changeling boy
To be my henchman.

    Queen.   Set your heart at rest.
The fairyland buys not the child of me.
His mother was a vot'ress of my order;   125
And in the spiced Indian air, by night,
Full often hath she gossiped by my side,
And sat with me on Neptune's yellow sands,
Marking the embarked traders on the flood;
When we have laughed to see the sails conceive   130
And grow big-bellied with the wanton wind;
Which she, with pretty and with swimming gait
Following (her womb then rich with my young squire)
Would imitate, and sail upon the land
To fetch me trifles, and return again,   135
As from a voyage, rich with merchandise.
But she, being mortal, of that boy did die,
And for her sake do I rear up her boy,
And for her sake I will not part with him.

    Ob. How long within this wood intend you stay?   140
    Queen. Perchance till after Theseus' wedding day.
If you will patiently dance in our round
And see our moonlight revels, go with us.
If not, shun me, and I will spare your haunts.

148. **shalt not from**: shall not depart from.

151. **Since**: meaning "when."

161. **a fair Vestal, throned by the West**: this is generally believed to be Shakespeare's compliment to Queen Elizabeth, the Virgin Queen.

164. **might**: could.

171. **love-in-idleness**: a fanciful name for the pansy.

174. **or . . . or**: either . . . or.

Mermaids
From Cartari, *Imagini dellı Dei de gl'Antichi* (1609).

    Ob. Give me that boy, and I will go with thee.   145
    Queen. Not for thy fairy kingdom. Fairies, away!
We shall chide downright if I longer stay.
                     Exeunt [*Titania and her Train*].
    Ob. Well, go thy way. Thou shalt not from this grove
Till I torment thee for this injury.
My gentle Puck, come hither. Thou rememb'rest   150
Since once I sat upon a promontory
And heard a mermaid, on a dolphin's back,
Uttering such dulcet and harmonious breath
That the rude sea grew civil at her song,
And certain stars shot madly from their spheres   155
To hear the sea-maid's music.
    Puck.   I remember.
    Ob. That very time I saw (but thou couldst not),
Flying between the cold moon and the earth,
Cupid, all armed. A certain aim he took   160
At a fair Vestal, throned by the West,
And loosed his love-shaft smartly from his bow,
As it should pierce a hundred thousand hearts.
But I might see young Cupid's fiery shaft
Quenched in the chaste beams of the wat'ry moon,   165
And the imperial vot'ress passed on,
In maiden meditation, fancy-free.
Yet marked I where the bolt of Cupid fell.
It fell upon a little Western flower,
Before milk-white, now purple with love's wound,   170
And maidens call it love-in-idleness.
Fetch me that flow'r; the herb I showed thee once.
The juice of it, on sleeping eyelids laid,
Will make or man or woman madly dote

177. **the Leviathan:** a whale. The Biblical Leviathan was so identified in Shakespeare's time.

194. **slay . . . slayeth:** an emendation suggested by Styan Thirlby for "stay . . . stayeth" in the early texts.

196. **wood within this wood:** the first **wood** means "out of one's mind," "enraged," or "furiously angry," from the Anglo-Saxon *wod*.

199. **adamant:** loadstone, magnet.

200-1. **iron . . . steel:** that is, instead of being hardhearted, I am tenderhearted and faithful; **Leave you:** abandon.

Upon the next live creature that it sees.   175
Fetch me this herb, and be thou here again
Ere the Leviathan can swim a league.
    Puck. I'll put a girdle round about the earth
In forty minutes.   [*Exit.*]
    Ob.   Having once this juice,   180
I'll watch Titania when she is asleep
And drop the liquor of it in her eyes.
The next thing then she, waking, looks upon
(Be it on lion, bear, or wolf, or bull,
On meddling monkey, or on busy ape)   185
She shall pursue it with the soul of love.
And ere I take this charm from off her sight
(As I can take it with another herb)
I'll make her render up her page to me.
But who comes here? I am invisible,   190
And I will overhear their conference.

Enter *Demetrius, Helena* following him.

    Dem. I love thee not; therefore pursue me not.
Where is Lysander and fair Hermia?
The one I'll slay, the other slayeth me.
Thou told'st me they were stol'n unto this wood;   195
And here am I, and wood within this wood
Because I cannot meet my Hermia.
Hence, get thee gone, and follow me no more!
    Hel. You draw me, you hardhearted adamant!
But yet you draw not iron, for my heart   200
Is true as steel. Leave you your power to draw,
And I shall have no power to follow you.
    Dem. Do I entice you? Do I speak you fair?

Apollo and Daphne.
From Ovid, *Metamorphoses* (1509).

218. impeach: stain the reputation of.

222. desert: wild.

224. Your virtue is my privilege: your powerful attractions give me such license; **for that:** because.

228. respect: regard; see I. [i.] 162.

231. brakes: thickets.

235. Apollo . . . and Daphne: the god Apollo fell in love with the nymph Daphne and pursued her until she appealed desperately for help and was changed to a laurel tree, as told in Ovid's *Metamorphoses*, Book I.

Or rather do I not in plainest truth
Tell you I do not nor I cannot love you?   205
　　Hel. And even for that do I love you the more.
I am your spaniel; and, Demetrius,
The more you beat me, I will fawn on you.
Use me but as your spaniel—spurn me, strike me,
Neglect me, lose me; only give me leave   210
(Unworthy as I am) to follow you.
What worser place can I beg in your love
(And yet a place of high respect with me)
Than to be used as you use your dog?
　　Dem. Tempt not too much the hatred of my spirit,   215
For I am sick when I do look on thee.
　　Hel. And I am sick when I look not on you.
　　Dem. You do impeach your modesty too much
To leave the city and commit yourself
Into the hands of one that loves you not;   220
To trust the opportunity of night
And the ill counsel of a desert place
With the rich worth of your virginity.
　　Hel. Your virtue is my privilege: for that
It is not night when I do see your face,   225
Therefore I think I am not in the night;
Nor doth this wood lack worlds of company,
For you, in my respect, are all the world:
Then how can it be said I am alone
When all the world is here to look on me?   230
　　Dem. I'll run from thee and hide me in the brakes,
And leave thee to the mercy of wild beasts.
　　Hel. The wildest hath not such a heart as you.
Run when you will, the story shall be changed:
Apollo flies, and Daphne holds the chase;   235

A griffon.

From Capaccio,
Delle Imprese Trattato (1592).

236. **griffon**: a mythological creature with the head and wings of an eagle and a lion's body.

237. **bootless**: vain, see II. [i.] 37.

239. **stay thy questions**: remain to be engaged in conversation.

240-1. **do not believe/ But**: do not think otherwise but that; be assured that.

244. **Your wrongs**: the wrong you have done me in winning my love and then spurning me.

255. **oxlips**: a variety of primrose, with a larger flower than the cowslip.

256. **woodbine**: a name applied to the common honeysuckle, but at IV. [i.] 41 Shakespeare refers to it in company with honeysuckle; he may therefore have called another twining plant by this name.

257. **eglantine**: the sweetbrier, *Rosa eglanteria*.

261. **Weed**: garment; see II. [ii.] 71.

23

The dove pursues the griffon; the mild hind
Makes speed to catch the tiger—bootless speed,
When cowardice pursues, and valor flies!
 Dem. I will not stay thy questions. Let me go!
Or if thou follow me, do not believe   240
But I shall do thee mischief in the wood.
 Hel. Ay, in the temple, in the town, the field,
You do me mischief. Fie, Demetrius!
Your wrongs do set a scandal on my sex.
We cannot fight for love, as men may do;   245
We should be wooed, and were not made to woo.
         [Exit Demetrius.]
I'll follow thee, and make a heaven of hell,
To die upon the hand I love so well.   *Exit.*
 Ob. Fare thee well, nymph. Ere he do leave this grove,
Thou shalt fly him, and he shall seek thy love.   250

     [Re-]enter *Puck.*

Hast thou the flower there? Welcome, wanderer.
 Puck. Ay, there it is.
 Ob.   I pray thee give it me.
I know a bank where the wild thyme blows,
Where oxlips and the nodding violet grows,   255
Quite over-canopied with luscious woodbine,
With sweet musk-roses, and with eglantine.
There sleeps Titania sometime of the night,
Lulled in these flowers with dances and delight;
And there the snake throws her enamelled skin,   260
Weed wide enough to wrap a fairy in;
And with the juice of this I'll streak her eyes
And make her full of hateful fantasies.

II. [ii.] Titania is sung to sleep by fairy attendants and has her eyes anointed by Oberon. Lysander and Hermia, weary from their exertions, choose a spot near Titania's flowery bed to rest and are discovered by Puck, who takes Lysander for the man described by Oberon and anoints his eyes. Helena comes in pursuing Demetrius, who makes his escape. Lysander is awakened by their noise and since Helena is the object his eye first lights upon, he immediately declares his passion for her. Helena feels that she is being mocked and runs away, pursued by Lysander, and Hermia awakens from a nightmare to find herself alone.

━━━━━━━━━━━━━━━━

1. **roundel:** a dance in a circle or ring, from Old French *rondele*.

4. **reremice:** bats.

7. **quaint:** clever.

8. **offices:** duties.

Take thou some of it and seek through this grove.
A sweet Athenian lady is in love   265
With a disdainful youth: anoint his eyes,
But do it when the next thing he espies
May be the lady. Thou shalt know the man
By the Athenian garments he hath on.
Effect it with some care, that he may prove   270
More fond on her than she upon her love;
And look thou meet me ere the first cock crow.
   Puck. Fear not, my lord; your servant shall do so.
                                    Exeunt.

[Scene II. Another part of the wood.]

Enter *Titania, Queen of Fairies,* with her *Train.*

   Queen. Come, now a roundel and a fairy song;
Then, for the third part of a minute, hence—
Some to kill cankers in the musk-rose buds,
Some war with reremice for their leathern wings,
To make my small elves coats, and some keep back   5
The clamorous owl, that nightly hoots and wonders
At our quaint spirits. Sing me now asleep.
Then to your offices, and let me rest.

Fairies sing.

   1. Fai. You spotted snakes with double tongue,
       Thorny hedgehogs, be not seen;   10

The fairy sentinel.
Designed by Paul Konewka.

13. **Philomel:** the nightingale, the transformed Philomela of Greek mythology; see Ovid, *Metamorphoses*, Book VI.

30. **ounce:** a member of the cat family; originally a lynx.

31. **Pard:** panther.

Newts and blindworms, do no wrong,
Come not near our Fairy Queen.

[*All.*]   Philomel, with melody
Sing in our sweet lullaby;
Lulla, lulla, lullaby; lulla, lulla, lullaby;   15
Never harm,
Nor spell nor charm
Come our lovely lady nigh.
So good night, with lullaby.

1. Fai.   Weaving spiders, come not here;   20
Hence, you long-legged spinners, hence!
Beetles black, approach not near;
Worm nor snail, do no offense.

[*All.*]   Philomel, with melody, &c.

                                    She sleeps.
2. Fai.   Hence, away! Now all is well.   25
One aloof stand sentinel.

                            [*Exeunt Fairies.*]

Enter *Oberon,* [and squeezes the flower on *Titania's*
eyelids].

Ob.   What thou seest when thou dost wake,
Do it for thy true-love take;
Love and languish for his sake.
Be it ounce or cat or bear,   30
Pard, or boar with bristled hair
In thy eye that shall appear
When thou wak'st, it is thy dear.
Wake when some vile thing is near.   [*Exit.*]

36. **troth:** truthfully.

42. **troth:** pledged faith.

45. **take the sense . . . of my innocence:** don't misinterpret what is really my innocence in proposing an impropriety.

46. **Love takes the meaning in love's conference:** that is, true lovers always understand each other.

52. **I do not lie:** that is, I play no false part in lying beside you as your faithful lover.

54. **beshrew:** curse, literally, though used with less emphatic meaning.

57. **in humane modesty:** modestly, as befits civilized beings.

Enter *Lysander* and *Hermia*.

Lys. Fair love, you faint with wand'ring in the wood;   35
And to speak troth, I have forgot our way.
We'll rest us, Hermia, if you think it good,
And tarry for the comfort of the day.
    Her. Be it so, Lysander. Find you out a bed;
For I upon this bank will rest my head.   40
    Lys. One turf shall serve as pillow for us both;
One heart, one bed, two bosoms, and one troth.
    Her. Nay, good Lysander; for my sake, my dear,
Lie further off yet, do not lie so near.
    Lys. O, take the sense, sweet, of my innocence!   45
Love takes the meaning in love's conference.
I mean that my heart unto yours is knit,
So that but one heart we can make of it;
Two bosoms interchained with an oath;
So then two bosoms and a single troth.   50
Then by your side no bed-room me deny;
For lying so, Hermia, I do not lie.
    Her. Lysander riddles very prettily.
Now much beshrew my manners and my pride
If Hermia meant to say Lysander lied!   55
But, gentle friend, for love and courtesy
Lie further off, in humane modesty,
Such separation as may well be said
Becomes a virtuous bachelor and a maid,
So far be distant; and good night, sweet friend,   60
Thy love ne'er alter till thy sweet life end!
    Lys. Amen, amen, to that fair prayer say I,
And then end life when I end loyalty!

Demetrius and Helena.
Designed by Paul Konewka.

68. **approve**: demonstrate.
71. **Weeds**: garments; see II. [i.] 261.
79. **owe**: possess.
86. **darkling**: in the dark.

Here is my bed. Sleep give thee all his rest!
  Her. With half that wish the wisher's eyes be pressed! 65
                                They sleep.

Enter Puck.

Puck. Through the forest have I gone,
    But Athenian found I none
    On whose eyes I might approve
    This flower's force in stirring love.
    Night and silence! Who is here? 70
    Weeds of Athens he doth wear.
    This is he (my master said)
    Despised the Athenian maid;
    And here the maiden, sleeping sound
    On the dank and dirty ground. 75
    Pretty soul! she durst not lie
    Near this lack-love, this kill-courtesy.
    Churl, upon thy eyes I throw
    All the power this charm doth owe.
    When thou wak'st, let love forbid 80
    Sleep his seat on thy eyelid.
    So awake when I am gone;
    For I must now to Oberon.   *Exit.*

Enter Demetrius and Helena, running.

Hel. Stay, though thou kill me, sweet Demetrius.
Dem. I charge thee, hence, and do not haunt me thus. 85
Hel. O, wilt thou darkling leave me? Do not so.
Dem. Stay, on thy peril! I alone will go.   *Exit.*
Hel. O, I am out of breath in this fond chase!

89. **grace:** the granting of my prayer (that I should please Demetrius).

97. **as:** as though I were.

99. **sphery:** starry.

105. **Transparent:** radiantly beautiful, diffusing beauty as the sun does its rays.

115. **raven . . . dove:** an unfavorable comparison between the brunette and blond complexions of Hermia and Helena, as well as their dispositions.

116. **will:** amorous desire.

The more my prayer, the lesser is my grace.
Happy is Hermia, wheresoe'er she lies;   90
For she hath blessed and attractive eyes.
How came her eyes so bright? Not with salt tears.
If so, my eyes are oft'ner washed than hers.
No, no! I am as ugly as a bear;
For beasts that meet me run away for fear.   95
Therefore no marvel though Demetrius
Do, as a monster, fly my presence thus.
What wicked and dissembling glass of mine
Made me compare with Hermia's sphery eyne?
But who is here? Lysander! on the ground?   100
Dead, or asleep? I see no blood, no wound.
Lysander, if you live, good sir, awake.
  Lys. [*Waking*] And run through fire I will for thy sweet
    sake.
Transparent Helena! Nature shows art,   105
That through thy bosom makes me see thy heart.
Where is Demetrius? O, how fit a word
Is that vile name to perish on my sword!
  Hel. Do not say so, Lysander; say not so.
What though he love your Hermia? Lord, what though? 110
Yet Hermia still loves you; then be content.
  Lys. Content with Hermia? No! I do repent
The tedious minutes I with her have spent.
Not Hermia, but Helena I love.
Who will not change a raven for a dove?   115
The will of man is by his reason swayed;
And reason says you are the worthier maid.
Things growing are not ripe until their season;
So I, being young, till now ripe not to reason;
And touching now the point of human skill,   120

129. **flout**: mock.
130. **good sooth**: truly.

Reason becomes the marshal to my will
And leads me to your eyes; where I o'erlook
Love's stories, written in Love's richest book.
    Hel. Wherefore was I to this keen mockery born?
When at your hands did I deserve this scorn?   125
Is't not enough, is't not enough, young man,
That I did never, no, nor never can,
Deserve a sweet look from Demetrius' eye,
But you must flout my insufficiency?
Good troth, you do me wrong! good sooth, you do!   130
In such disdainful manner me to woo.
But fare you well. Perforce I must confess
I thought you lord of more true gentleness.
O, that a lady, of one man refused,
Should of another therefore be abused!   *Exit.* 135
    Lys. She sees not Hermia. Hermia, sleep thou there,
And never mayst thou come Lysander near!
For, as a surfeit of the sweetest things
The deepest loathing to the stomach brings,
Or as the heresies that men do leave   140
Are hated most of those they did deceive,
So thou, my surfeit and my heresy,
Of all be hated, but the most of me!
And, all my powers, address your love and might
To honor Helen and to be her knight!   *Exit.* 145
    Her. [*Waking*] Help me, Lysander, help me! Do thy
      best
To pluck this crawling serpent from my breast!
Ay me, for pity, what a dream was here!
Lysander, look how I do quake with fear.   150
Methought a serpent eat my heart away,
And you sat smiling at his cruel prey.

156. **of all loves:** in the name of love; if you love me at all.

Lysander! What, removed? Lysander! lord!
What, out of hearing? gone? no sound, no word?
Alack, where are you? Speak, an if you hear.   155
Speak, of all loves! I swoon almost with fear.
No? Then I well perceive you are not nigh:
Either death or you I'll find immediately.

Exit.

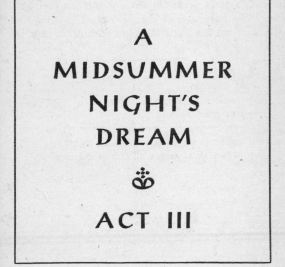

A
MIDSUMMER
NIGHT'S
DREAM

❧

ACT III

III. [i.] The artisans meet to rehearse their interlude and Puck comes upon them. He frightens them away and gives Bottom an ass's head. His comrades all flee him when they see his transformation, but Bottom, blissfully unconscious of his altered appearance, walks manfully up and down, singing defiantly. Titania is awakened by the song, is immediately enamored of the bewitched Bottom, and summons her fairy attendants to wait upon him.

⸺⸺⸺⸺⸺⸺

2. **Pat:** exactly.

4. **tiring house:** dressing room.

7. **bully:** good fellow.

12. **By'r lakin:** by our little lady (the Virgin Mary); **parlous:** perilous, of serious degree.

13-4. **when all is done:** all things considered.

ACT III

[Scene I. The same. Titania lying asleep.]

Enter the Clowns—[*Quince, Snug, Bottom, Flute, Snout and Starveling*].

Bot. Are we all met?

Quince. Pat, pat; and here's a marvelous convenient place for our rehearsal. This green plot shall be our stage, this hawthorn brake our tiring house, and we will do it in action as we will do it before the duke. 5

Bot. Peter Quince!

Quince. What sayest thou, bully Bottom?

Bot. There are things in this Comedy of Pyramus and Thisby that will never please. First, Pyramus must draw a sword to kill himself; which the ladies cannot abide. How 10 answer you that?

Snout. By'r lakin, a parlous fear!

Starv. I believe we must leave the killing out, when all is done.

Bot. Not a whit: I have a device to make all well. 15 Write me a prologue; and let the prologue seem to say, we will do no harm with our swords, and that Pyramus is not killed indeed; and for the more better assurance, tell them

31

22. **in eight and six**: in verse consisting of alternate lines of eight and six syllables respectively, an old-fashioned form of jog-trot verse.

35. **defect**: effect, a characteristic comic blunder.

39. **it were pity of my life**: it would be at peril of my life.

that I Pyramus am not Pyramus, but Bottom the weaver.
This will put them out of fear.   20

Quince. Well, we will have such a prologue, and it shall
be written in eight and six.

Bot. No, make it two more: let it be written in eight
and eight.

Snout. Will not the ladies be afeard of the lion?   25

Starv. I fear it, I promise you.

Bot. Masters, you ought to consider with yourselves, to
bring in (God shield us!) a lion among ladies is a most
dreadful thing. For there is not a more fearful wild-fowl
than your lion living; and we ought to look to't.   30

Snout. Therefore another prologue must tell he is not a
lion.

Bot. Nay, you must name his name, and half his face
must be seen through the lion's neck, and he himself must
speak through, saying thus, or to the same defect: 35
"Ladies"—or "Fair ladies, I would wish you"—or "I would
request you"—or "I would entreat you—not to fear, not to
tremble. My life for yours! If you think I come hither as
a lion, it were pity of my life. No! I am no such thing, I
am a man as other men are." And there, indeed, let him   40
name his name and tell them plainly he is Snug the joiner.

Quince. Well, it shall be so. But there is two hard
things: that is, to bring the moonlight into a chamber: for,
you know, Pyramus and Thisby meet by moonlight.

Snout. Doth the moon shine that night we play our   45
play?

Bot. A calendar, a calendar! Look in the almanac. Find
out moonshine, find out moonshine!

Quince. Yes, it doth shine that night.

54. **disfigure**: figure, portray.
62. **roughcast**: coarse plaster.
73. **toward**: in the offing.

Bot. Why, then may you leave a casement of the great   50
chamber window, where we play, open, and the moon
may shine in at the casement.

Quince. Ay; or else one must come in with a bush of
thorns and a lantern, and say he comes to disfigure, or to
present, the person of Moonshine. Then there is another   55
thing: we must have a wall in the great chamber; for
Pyramus and Thisby, says the story, did talk through the
chink of a wall.

Snout. You can never bring in a wall. What say you,
Bottom?   60

Bot. Some man or other must present Wall; and let him
have some plaster, or some loam, or some roughcast about
him, to signify wall; and let him hold his fingers thus; and
through that cranny shall Pyramus and Thisby whisper.

Quince. If that may be, then all is well. Come, sit   65
down, every mother's son, and rehearse your parts.
Pyramus, you begin. When you have spoken your speech,
enter into that brake; and so every one according to his
cue.

Enter [*Puck,*] *Robin* [*Goodfellow*].

Puck. What hempen homespuns have we swagg'ring   70
    here,
So near the cradle of the Fairy Queen?
What, a play toward? I'll be an auditor;
An actor too perhaps, if I see cause.

Quince. Speak, Pyramus. Thisby, stand forth.   75

Bot. (as Pyr.) Thisby, the flowers of odious savors
    sweet—

Quince. Odorous! odorous!

Ninus, first ruler of the Assyrians.
From *Promptuarii Iconum* . . . (1553).

90. **triumphant**: magnificent.
91. **juvenal**: youth; **eke**: also, in addition.
100. **fair**: handsome enough to urge a suit.

Bot. (as Pyr.) ——odors savors sweet;
So hath thy breath, my dearest Thisby dear.   80
But hark, a voice! Stay thou but here awhile,
And by-and-by I will to thee appear.   *Exit.*

Puck. A stranger Pyramus than e'er played here! [*Exit.*]

Flute. Must I speak now?

Quince. Ay, marry, must you; for you must understand 85
he goes but to see a noise that he heard, and is to come
again.

Flute (as This.) Most radiant Pyramus, most lily-white
   of hue,
Of color like the red rose on triumphant brier,   90
Most brisky juvenal, and eke most lovely Jew,
As true as truest horse, that yet would never tire,
I'll meet thee, Pyramus, at Ninny's tomb.

Quince. "Ninus' tomb," man! Why, you must not speak
that yet. That you answer to Pyramus. You speak all your 95
part at once, cues and all. Pyramus, enter. Your cue is
past; it is "never tire."

Flute (as This.) O—As true as truest horse, that yet
   would never tire.

[*Re-enter Puck, and Bottom as*] *Pyramus* with the
ass-head.

Bot. (as Pyr.) If I were fair, Thisby, I were only thine. 100

Quince. O monstrous! O strange! We are haunted.
Pray, masters! Fly, masters! Help!

          The Clowns all exeunt. [*Manet Bottom*].

Puck. I'll follow you; I'll lead you about a round,
Through bog, through bush, through brake, through brier:
Sometime a horse I'll be, sometime a hound,   105

"You see an ass-head of your own, do you?"
Designed by Paul Konewka.

113-14. **You see an ass-head of your own:** Bottom is unaware of his transformation; his reply to Snout means only that Snout is a fool in trying, as he thinks, to make a fool of him.

115-16. **translated:** transformed.

121. **woosel:** ousel, an English blackbird.

123. **throstle:** thrush.

124. **little quill:** reedy voice; a **quill** was a pipe-like musical instrument made of reed or cane.

A hog, a headless bear, sometime a fire;
And neigh, and bark, and grunt, and roar, and burn,
Like horse, hound, hog, bear, fire, at every turn.   *Exit.*
   Bot. Why do they run away? This is a knavery of them
to make me afeard.   110

[Re-]enter *Snout.*

   Snout. O Bottom, thou art changed! What do I see on
thee?
   Bot. What do you see? You see an ass-head of your
own, do you?
                                          [*Exit Snout.*]

[Re-]enter *Quince.*

   Quince. Bless thee, Bottom! bless thee! Thou art trans- 115
lated.   *Exit.*
   Bot. I see their knavery: this is to make an ass of me;
to fright me, if they could. But I will not stir from this
place, do what they can: I will walk up and down here,
and I will sing, that they shall hear I am not afraid.   120
                                          [*Sings.*]

      The woosel cock so black of hue,
         With orange-tawny bill,
      The throstle with his note so true,
         The wren with little quill—

   Tita. [*Waking*] What angel wakes me from my flow'ry 125
      bed?

128. **plain-song cuckoo**: the cuckoo sings a simple song, compared here to the religious plain song, an unvaried, simple melody.

129-30. **full many a man doth mark,/ And dares not answer nay**: "cuckoo" closely resembles the word "cuckold," the term for a man whose wife is unfaithful.

131. **set**: oppose.

133. **never so**: as never before.

143. **gleek**: mock, a reference to the satirical comments he has just made.

149. **rate**: rank.

150. **still**: always; see I. [i.] 217.

Bot. [*Sings.*]

> The finch, the sparrow, and the lark,
> The plain-song cuckoo gray,
> Whose note full many a man doth mark,
> And dares not answer nay.   130

For, indeed, who would set his wit to so foolish a bird?
Who would give a bird the lie, though he cry "cuckoo"
never so?

Tita. I pray thee, gentle mortal, sing again.
Mine ear is much enamored of thy note;   135
So is mine eye enthralled to thy shape;
And thy fair virtue's force (perforce) doth move me,
On the first view, to say, to swear, I love thee.

Bot. Methinks, mistress, you should have little reason
for that. And yet, to say the truth, reason and love keep 140
little company together nowadays. The more the pity that
some honest neighbors will not make them friends. Nay,
I can gleek, upon occasion.

Tita. Thou art as wise as thou art beautiful.

Bot. Not so, neither; but if I had wit enough to get out 145
of this wood, I have enough to serve mine own turn.

Tita. Out of this wood do not desire to go:
Thou shalt remain here, whether thou wilt or no.
I am a spirit of no common rate,
The summer still doth tend upon my state;   150
And I do love thee. Therefore go with me.
I'll give thee fairies to attend on thee;
And they shall fetch thee jewels from the deep,
And sing while thou on pressed flowers dost sleep;
And I will purge thy mortal grossness so   155

157. **Moth:** mote, a diminutive creature.

167. **humblebees:** bumblebees.

182-83. **make bold with you:** i.e., to stanch the blood, a traditional home remedy.

That thou shalt like an airy spirit go.
Peaseblossom! Cobweb! Moth! and Mustardseed!

Enter [the] four *Fairies.*

Peas. Ready.
Cob. And I.
Moth. And I.   160
Must. And I.
All. Where shall we go?
Tita. Be kind and courteous to this gentleman.
Hop in his walks and gambol in his eyes;
Feed him with apricocks and dewberries,   165
With purple grapes, green figs, and mulberries;
The honey-bags steal from the humblebees,
And for night tapers crop their waxen thighs,
And light them at the fiery glowworm's eyes,
To have my love to bed and to arise;   170
And pluck the wings from painted butterflies
To fan the moonbeams from his sleeping eyes.
Nod to him, elves, and do him courtesies.
Peas. Hail, mortal!
Cob. Hail!   175
Moth. Hail!
Must. Hail!
Bot. I cry your worships mercy, heartily. I beseech
your worship's name.
Cob. Cobweb.   180
Bot. I shall desire you of more acquaintance, good
Master Cobweb. If I cut my finger, I shall make bold with
you. Your name, honest gentleman?
Peas. Peaseblossom.

185. **Squash:** a green peapod.
186. **Peascod:** a ripe peapod.
191. **ox-beef:** for which mustard was a conventional accompaniment at table.

┄┄┄┄┄┄┄┄┄┄

III. [ii.] Puck reports his success to Oberon, who is displeased to find, when Demetrius and Hermia enter, that Puck has used the flower on the wrong Athenian. He dispatches Puck to find Helena and bring her into Demetrius' sight while he uses the magic flower on his eyes. Helena enters with Lysander, still declaring his love; Demetrius awakens and, charmed by the potent juice, makes his own passionate declarations to Helena. Hermia reappears and is bewildered by Lysander's desertion and his evident new devotion to Helena, while the latter thinks all three have conspired to make fun of her. Lysander and Demetrius threaten each other, while Hermia and Helena bicker. Finally, Puck lures Lysander and Demetrius away and, on instructions from Oberon, goes to seek an antidote to the love charm with which to restore Lysander's original love for Hermia. This done, Helena will have her Demetrius and Hermia and Lysander will be reconciled.

┄┄┄┄┄┄┄┄┄┄

3. **in extremity:** excessively.
5. **What night-rule now:** what's going on tonight.

Bot. I pray you, commend me to Mistress Squash, your 185
mother, and to Master Peascod, your father. Good Master
Peaseblossom, I shall desire you of more acquaintance too.
Your name, I beseech you, sir?

Must. Mustardseed.

Bot. Good Master Mustardseed, I know your patience 190
well. That same cowardly, giant-like ox-beef hath de-
voured many a gentleman of your house. I promise you
your kindred hath made my eyes water ere now. I desire
you of more acquaintance, good Master Mustardseed.

Tita. Come wait upon him; lead him to my bower.   195
The moon, methinks, looks with a wat'ry eye;
And when she weeps, weeps every little flower,
Lamenting some enforced chastity.
Tie up my love's tongue, bring him silently.

                                        Exeunt.

[Scene II. Another part of the wood.]

Enter [*Oberon,*] *King of Fairies.*

Ob. I wonder if Titania be awaked;
Then, what it was that next came in her eye,
Which she must dote on in extremity.

Enter *Puck.*

Here comes my messenger. How now, mad spirit?
What night-rule now about this haunted grove?   5

7. **close:** secret.

9. **patches:** fools; **mechanicals:** artisans.

13. **barren sort:** empty-headed lot.

17. **nole:** head, from the Old English *knoll.*

21. **choughs:** jackdaws; **in sort:** in company together.

28. **Made senseless things begin to do them wrong:** imagined injuries from inanimate objects.

30. **from yielders all things catch:** that is, those who have abandoned all defenses become universal targets of attack.

36. **latched:** caught, snared.

Puck. My mistress with a monster is in love.
Near to her close and consecrated bower,
While she was in her dull and sleeping hour,
A crew of patches, rude mechanicals,
That work for bread upon Athenian stalls,   10
Were met together to rehearse a play,
Intended for great Theseus' nuptial day.
The shallowest thickskin of that barren sort,
Who Pyramus presented in their sport,
Forsook his scene and ent'red in a brake.   15
When I did him at this advantage take,
An ass's nole I fixed on his head.
Anon his Thisby must be answered,
And forth my mimic comes. When they him spy,
As wild geese that the creeping fowler eye,   20
Or russet-pated choughs, many in sort,
Rising and cawing at the gun's report,
Sever themselves and madly sweep the sky;
So at his sight away his fellows fly;
And, at our stamp, here o'er and o'er one falls;   25
He murder cries and help from Athens calls.
Their sense thus weak, lost with their fears thus strong,
Made senseless things begin to do them wrong;
For briers and thorns at their apparel snatch;
Some, sleeves—some, hats; from yielders all things catch.   30
I led them on in this distracted fear
And left sweet Pyramus translated there;
When in that moment (so it came to pass)
Titania waked, and straightway loved an ass.
    Ob. This falls out better than I could devise.   35
But hast thou yet latched the Athenian's eyes
With the love-juice, as I did bid thee do?

APOLLO

Phoebus Apollo in his chariot.
From R. Whitcombe, *Janua Divorum* . . . (1678).

53. **whole**: solid.

55. **Her brother's**: Phoebus'. The moon and sun were brother and sister in classical mythology; **the Antipodes**: the other side of the earth and its inhabitants.

57. **dead**: deadly.

62. **What's this to**: how does this concern.

Puck. I took him sleeping (that is finished too)
And the Athenian woman by his side,
That, when he waked, of force she must be eyed.   40

Enter *Demetrius* and *Hermia.*

Ob. Stand close. This is the same Athenian.
Puck. This is the woman, but not this the man.
Dem. O, why rebuke you him that loves you so?
Lay breath so bitter on your bitter foe.
   Her. Now I but chide; but I should use thee worse,   45
For thou, I fear, hast given me cause to curse.
If thou hast slain Lysander in his sleep,
Being o'er shoes in blood, plunge in the deep,
And kill me too.
The sun was not so true unto the day   50
As he to me. Would he have stolen away
From sleeping Hermia? I'll believe as soon
This whole earth may be bored, and that the moon
May through the centre creep, and so displease
Her brother's noontide with the Antipodes.   55
It cannot be but thou hast murd'red him.
So should a murderer look, so dead, so grim.
   Dem. So should the murdered look, and so should I,
Pierced through the heart with your stern cruelty.
Yet you, the murderer, look as bright, as clear,   60
As yonder Venus in her glimmering sphere.
   Her. What's this to my Lysander? Where is he?
Ah, good Demetrius, wilt thou give him me?
   Dem. I had rather give his carcass to my hounds.
   Her. Out, dog! out, cur! Thou driv'st me past the   65
   bounds

70. **Durst thou**: would you dare.

71. **brave**: noble, splendid.

72. **worm**: snake.

75. **misprised**: mistaken.

81. **so**: Alexander Pope's emendation of "see" in the early texts.

85. **heaviness**: sadness.

86. **bankrout**: bankrupt.

88. **If for his tender here I make some stay**: if I wait here a bit to allow sleep to offer itself.

91. **misprision**: mistake; see l. 75 above.

93-4. **Then fate o'errules, that, one man holding troth,/ A million fail, confounding oath on oath**: do what we may, fate governs these matters so that only one man in a million is faithful in love; **confounding** means "destroying."

Of maiden's patience. Hast thou slain him then?
Henceforth be never numb'red among men!
O, once tell true! tell true, even for my sake!
Durst thou have looked upon him, being awake?   70
And hast thou killed him sleeping? O brave touch!
Could not a worm, an adder, do so much?
An adder did it; for with doubler tongue
Than thine (thou serpent!) never adder stung.

   Dem. You spend your passion on a misprised mood.   75
I am not guilty of Lysander's blood;
Nor is he dead, for aught that I can tell.

   Her. I pray thee, tell me then that he is well.

   Dem. An if I could, what should I get therefore?

   Her. A privilege never to see me more;   80
And from thy hated presence part I so.
See me no more, whether he be dead or no.   *Exit.*

   Dem. There is no following her in this fierce vein:
Here therefore for a while I will remain.
So sorrow's heaviness doth heavier grow   85
For debt that bankrout sleep doth sorrow owe;
Which now in some slight measure it will pay,
If for his tender here I make some stay.

                Lie down [*and sleep*].

   Ob. What hast thou done? Thou hast mistaken quite
And laid the love-juice on some true-love's sight.   90
Of thy misprision must perforce ensue
Some true-love turned, and not a false turned true.

   Puck. Then fate o'errules, that, one man holding troth,
A million fail, confounding oath on oath.

   Ob. About the wood go swifter than the wind,   95
And Helena of Athens look thou find.

97. **fancy-sick:** lovesick; **cheer:** face.

98. **With sighs of love, that costs the fresh blood dear:** a reference to the belief that sighing weakened the heart by drawing blood from it.

100. **against she do appear:** in preparation for her appearance.

115. **fond:** foolish; **pageant:** exhibition.

120. **sport alone:** unparalleled sport.

All fancy-sick she is, and pale of cheer
With sighs of love, that costs the fresh blood dear.
By some illusion see thou bring her here.
I'll charm his eyes against she do appear.   100
    Puck. I go, I go! Look how I go!
Swifter than an arrow from the Tartar's bow.   *Exit.*

Ob.   Flower of this purple dye,
         Hit with Cupid's archery,
         Sink in apple of his eye!   105
         When his love he doth espy,
         Let her shine as gloriously
         As the Venus of the sky.
         When thou wak'st, if she be by,
         Beg of her for remedy.   110

                    [Re-]enter *Puck.*

Puck. Captain of our fairy band,
         Helena is here at hand,
         And the youth, mistook by me,
         Pleading for a lover's fee.
         Shall we their fond pageant see?   115
         Lord, what fools these mortals be!

Ob.   Stand aside: the noise they make
         Will cause Demetrius to awake.

Puck. Then will two at once woo one.
         That must needs be sport alone;   120
         And those things do best please me
         That befall prepost'rously.

126. **all**: nothing but.

128. **badge of faith**: his tears prove his faith just as the badge on a servant's uniform indicates his allegiance to the family he serves.

129. **advance**: flaunt.

130. **When truth kills truth, O devilish-holy fray**: if his present vow is true, it kills the truth of his previous vow of love to Hermia, and a contest between false and true oaths makes a **devilish-holy fray**.

143. **Taurus**: a mountain range in Turkey.

Enter *Lysander* and *Helena*.

Lys. Why should you think that I should woo in scorn?
Scorn and derision never come in tears:
Look, when I vow, I weep; and vows so born,   125
In their nativity all truth appears.
How can these things in me seem scorn to you,
Bearing the badge of faith to prove them true?
  Hel. You do advance your cunning more and more.
When truth kills truth, O devilish-holy fray!   130
These vows are Hermia's. Will you give her o'er?
Weigh oath with oath, and you will nothing weigh.
Your vows to her and me, put in two scales,
Will even weigh, and both as light as tales.
  Lys. I had no judgment when to her I swore.   135
  Hel. Nor none, in my mind, now you give her o'er.
  Lys. Demetrius loves her, and he loves not you.
  Dem. [*Waking*] O Helen, goddess, nymph, perfect,
    divine!
To what, my love, shall I compare thine eyne?   140
Crystal is muddy. O, how ripe in show
Thy lips, those kissing cherries, tempting grow!
That pure congealed white, high Taurus' snow,
Fanned with the eastern wind, turns to a crow
When thou hold'st up thy hand: O, let me kiss   145
This princess of pure white, this seal of bliss!
  Hel. O spite! O hell! I see you all are bent
To set against me for your merriment.
If you were civil and knew courtesy,

152. **join in souls:** conspire.
159. **trim:** fine.
162. **extort:** extract forcibly.
171. **I will none:** I will have none of her.
178. **aby it dear:** buy it at great cost.

Hermia and Lysander.
Designed by Paul Konewka.

You would not do me thus much injury.   150
Can you not hate me, as I know you do,
But you must join in souls to mock me too?
If you were men, as men you are in show,
You would not use a gentle lady so;
To vow, and swear, and superpraise my parts,   155
When I am sure you hate me with your hearts.
You both are rivals, and love Hermia;
And now both rivals to mock Helena.
A trim exploit, a manly enterprise,
To conjure tears up in a poor maid's eyes   160
With your derision! None of noble sort
Would so offend a virgin and extort
A poor soul's patience, all to make you sport.
   Lys. You are unkind, Demetrius. Be not so!
For you love Hermia; this you know I know;   165
And here, with all good will, with all my heart,
In Hermia's love I yield you up my part;
And yours of Helena to me bequeath,
Whom I do love, and will do to my death.
   Hel. Never did mockers waste more idle breath.   170
   Dem. Lysander, keep thy Hermia, I will none:
If e'er I loved her, all that love is gone.
My heart to her but as guestwise sojourned,
And now to Helen is it home returned,
There to remain.   175
   Lys.   Helen, it is not so.
   Dem. Disparage not the faith thou dost not know,
Lest, to thy peril, thou aby it dear.
Look where thy love comes; yonder is thy dear.

191. **oes:** circles, or circular spangles, like sequins.

198. **Injurious:** insulting.

200. **bait:** torment.

206. **artificial:** related to the word "artificer," craftsman.

Enter *Hermia.*

Her. Dark night, that from the eye his function takes, 180
The ear more quick of apprehension makes.
Wherein it doth impair the seeing sense,
It pays the hearing double recompense.
Thou art not by mine eye, Lysander, found;
Mine ear, I thank it, brought me to thy sound. 185
But why unkindly didst thou leave me so?
　Lys. Why should he stay whom love doth press to go?
　Her. What love could press Lysander from my side?
　Lys. Lysander's love, that would not let him bide,
Fair Helena; who more engilds the night 190
Than all yon fiery oes and eyes of light.
Why seek'st thou me? Could not this make thee know,
The hate I bare thee made me leave thee so?
　Her. You speak not as you think; it cannot be.
　Hel. Lo, she is one of this confederacy! 195
Now I perceive they have conjoined all three
To fashion this false sport in spite of me.
Injurious Hermia! most ungrateful maid!
Have you conspired, have you with these contrived
To bait me with this foul derision? 200
Is all the counsel that we two have shared,
The sisters' vows, the hours that we have spent
When we have chid the hasty-footed time
For parting us—O, is all forgot?
All schooldays friendship, childhood innocence? 205
We, Hermia, like two artificial gods,
Have with our needles created both one flower,
Both on one sampler, sitting on one cushion,

211. **incorporate:** combined into one body.

216-17. **Two of the first, like coats in heraldry,/ Due but to one:** two bodies controlled by one heart, like the arms of a man and his wife which are combined to symbolize their union.

218. **rent:** tear.

223. **amazed:** struck dumb.

235. **so in grace:** so popular.

236. **hung upon with love:** caressed.

Both warbling of one song, both in one key;
As if our hands, our sides, voices, and minds   210
Had been incorporate. So we grew together,
Like to a double cherry, seeming parted,
But yet an union in partition—
Two lovely berries moulded on one stem;
So, with two seeming bodies, but one heart;   215
Two of the first, like coats in heraldry,
Due but to one, and crowned with one crest.
And will you rent our ancient love asunder,
To join with men in scorning your poor friend?
It is not friendly, 'tis not maidenly!   220
Our sex, as well as I, may chide you for it,
Though I alone do feel the injury.

   Her. I am amazed at your passionate words.
I scorn you not. It seems that you scorn me.

   Hel. Have you not set Lysander, as in scorn,   225
To follow me and praise my eyes and face?
And made your other love, Demetrius
(Who even but now did spurn me with his foot),
To call me goddess, nymph, divine, and rare,
Precious, celestial? Wherefore speaks he this   230
To her he hates? And wherefore doth Lysander
Deny your love (so rich within his soul)
And tender me (forsooth) affection,
But by your setting on, by your consent?
What though I be not so in grace as you,   235
So hung upon with love, so fortunate;
But miserable most, to love unloved?
This you should pity rather than despise.

   Her. I understand not what you mean by this.

240. **persever:** persevere; **sad:** grave.

241. **mouths:** grimaces.

243. **carried:** carried off.

244. **grace:** goodness.

245. **such an argument:** the subject of such a tale; such a figure of fun.

254. **prayers:** Theobald's emendation for "praise" in the early texts.

262. **Ethiope:** another reference to Hermia's dark coloring.

263-5. **No, no, etc.:** the reading at this point is confused and the arrangement of the text here follows a suggestion by G. E. Jaisey in *Notes and Queries*, 8th Series, III, 102.

267. **thou cat, thou burr:** directed at Hermia, who is clinging to him.

Hel. Ay, do! persever, counterfeit sad looks,   240
Make mouths upon me when I turn my back,
Wink each at other, hold the sweet jest up:
This sport, well carried, shall be chronicled.
If you have any pity, grace, or manners,
You would not make me such an argument.   245
But fare ye well. 'Tis partly my own fault,
Which death or absence soon shall remedy.

Lys. Stay, gentle Helena; hear my excuse,
My love, my life, my soul, fair Helena!

Hel. O excellent!   250

Her.   Sweet, do not scorn her so.

Dem. If she cannot entreat, I can compel.

Lys. Thou canst compel no more than she entreat.
Thy threats have no more strength than her weak prayers.
Helen, I love thee; by my life, I do!   255
I swear by that which I will lose for thee
To prove him false that says I love thee not.

Dem. I say I love thee more than he can do.

Lys. If thou say so, withdraw and prove it too.

Dem. Quick, come!   260

Her.   Lysander, whereto tends all this?

Lys. Away, you Ethiope!

Her.   No, no; he'll—

Dem. Seem to break loose, take on as you would fol-
    low,   265
But yet come not. You are a tame man, go!

Lys. Hang off, thou cat, thou burr! Vile thing, let loose,
Or I will shake thee from me like a serpent!

Her. Why are you grown so rude? What change is this,
Sweet love?   270

277. **A weak bond**: i.e., a woman—Hermia.

284. **Since night . . . since night you left me**: you loved me as recently as nightfall, but since nightfall you have deserted me.

292. **canker blossom**: the wild rose called "dog rose" in England was also known by this name, but it is likely that Hermia is comparing Helena to a canker which spoils the rose's beauty.

299. **puppet**: Hermia is not only a **counterfeit** but a miniature one to Helena, who is taller than she.

Lys.   Thy love? Out, tawny Tartar, out!
Out, loathed med'cine! O hated potion, hence!
    Her. Do you not jest?
    Hel.   Yes, sooth! and so do you.
    Lys. Demetrius, I will keep my word with thee.   275
    Dem. I would I had your bond; for I perceive
A weak bond holds you. I'll not trust your word.
    Lys. What, should I hurt her, strike her, kill her dead?
Although I hate her, I'll not harm her so.
    Her. What, can you do me greater harm than hate?   280
Hate me? Wherefore? O me! what news, my love?
Am not I Hermia? Are not you Lysander?
I am as fair now as I was erewhile.
Since night you loved me; yet since night you left me.
Why then, you left me (O, the gods forbid!)   285
In earnest, shall I say?
    Lys.   Ay, by my life!
And never did desire to see thee more.
Therefore be out of hope, of question, doubt;
Be certain, nothing truer, 'tis no jest   290
That I do hate thee, and love Helena.
    Her. O me! you juggler! you canker blossom!
You thief of love! What, have you come by night
And stol'n my love's heart from him?
    Hel.   Fine, i' faith!   295
Have you no modesty, no maiden shame,
No touch of bashfulness? What, will you tear
Impatient answers from my gentle tongue?
Fie, fie! you counterfeit, you puppet you!
    Her. Puppet? Why, so! Ay, that way goes the game.   300
Now I perceive that she hath made compare
Between our statures; she hath urged her height,

311. **curst**: quarrelsome.
313. **right**: true.
329. **fond**: foolish; see III. [ii.] 115.

And with her personage, her tall personage,
Her height (forsooth), she hath prevailed with him.
And are you grown so high in his esteem   305
Because I am so dwarfish and so low?
How low am I, thou painted maypole? Speak!
How low am I? I am not yet so low
But that my nails can reach unto thine eyes.

Hel. I pray you, though you mock me, gentlemen,   310
Let her not hurt me. I was never curst;
I have no gift at all in shrewishness;
I am a right maid for my cowardice.
Let her not strike me. You perhaps may think,
Because she is something lower than myself,   315
That I can match her.

    Her.   Lower? Hark again!

    Hel. Good Hermia, do not be so bitter with me.
I evermore did love you, Hermia,
Did ever keep your counsels, never wronged you;   320
Save that, in love unto Demetrius,
I told him of your stealth unto this wood.
He followed you; for love I followed him;
But he hath chid me hence, and threat'ned me
To strike me, spurn me; nay, to kill me too.   325
And now, so you will let me quiet go,
To Athens will I bear my folly back
And follow you no further. Let me go.
You see how simple and how fond I am.

    Her. Why, get you gone! Who is't that hinders you?   330

    Hel. A foolish heart, that I leave here behind.

    Her. What, with Lysander?

    Hel.   With Demetrius.

    Lys. Be not afraid, she shall not harm thee, Helena.

335. **though you take her part:** a jeer at Lysander's worth as a defender.

336. **keen:** sharp; **shrewd:** shrewish.

340. **suffer:** permit.

343. **minimus:** tiniest of beings. Theobald complained of this passage, saying that Shakespeare would not have used bad Latin by applying a noun with a masculine ending to Hermia; **of hind'ring knotgrass made:** nourished on knotgrass, which supposedly stunted growth if eaten.

348. **intend:** offer.

350. **aby:** pay for; see l. 178.

355. **coil:** trouble, to-do; **'long:** because.

Dem. No, sir, she shall not, though you take her part.   335
    Hel. O, when she is angry, she is keen and shrewd!
She was a vixen when she went to school,
And though she be but little, she is fierce.
    Her. "Little" again? nothing but "low" and "little"?
Why will you suffer her to flout me thus?   340
Let me come to her.
    Lys.   Get you gone, you dwarf!
You minimus, of hind'ring knotgrass made!
You bead, you acorn!
    Dem.   You are too officious   345
In her behalf that scorns your services.
Let her alone. Speak not of Helena;
Take not her part; for if thou dost intend
Never so little show of love to her,
Thou shalt aby it.   350
    Lys.   Now she holds me not.
Now follow, if thou dar'st, to try whose right,
Of thine or mine, is most in Helena.
    Dem. Follow? Nay, I'll go with thee, cheek by jowl.
                    Exeunt Lysander and Demetrius.
    Her. You, mistress, all this coil is 'long of you.   355
Nay, go not back.
    Hel.   I will not trust you, I,
Nor longer stay in your curst company.
Your hands than mine are quicker for a fray;
My legs are longer though, to run away.   [*Exit.*]   360
    Her. I am amazed, and know not what to say.   *Exit.*
    Ob. This is thy negligence. Still thou mistak'st,
Or else committ'st thy knaveries wilfully.
    Puck. Believe me, king of shadows, I mistook.
Did not you tell me I should know the man   365

Aurora, goddess of the dawn.
From Cartari, *Imagini delli Dei de gl'Antichi* (1615).

369. **so did sort**: came out this way.

372. **Hie**: hurry.

373. **welkin**: sky.

374. **Acheron**: originally a river in Hades over which the souls of the dead were ferried, also applied to Hell generally.

375. **testy**: touchy.

384. **virtuous property**: excellent (both good and powerful) quality.

385. **his**: its; that is, the might of the liquor.

386. **wonted**: accustomed (as before).

387. **derision**: mockery; the sport we have made of them.

390. **With league whose date till death shall never end**: that is, united by vows of love which shall last till death.

51

By the Athenian garments he had on?
And so far blameless proves my enterprise
That I have 'nointed an Athenian's eyes;
And so far am I glad it so did sort,
As this their jangling I esteem a sport.   370
   Ob. Thou seest these lovers seek a place to fight.
Hie therefore, Robin, overcast the night.
The starry welkin cover thou anon
With drooping fog as black as Acheron,
And lead these testy rivals so astray   375
As one come not within another's way.
Like to Lysander sometime frame thy tongue,
Then stir Demetrius up with bitter wrong;
And sometime rail thou like Demetrius.
And from each other look thou lead them thus   380
Till o'er their brows death-counterfeiting sleep
With leaden legs and batty wings doth creep.
Then crush this herb into Lysander's eye;
Whose liquor hath this virtuous property,
To take from thence all error with his might   385
And make his eyeballs roll with wonted sight.
When they next wake, all this derision
Shall seem a dream and fruitless vision;
And back to Athens shall the lovers wend
With league whose date till death shall never end.   390
Whiles I in this affair do thee employ,
I'll to my queen and beg her Indian boy;
And then I will her charmed eye release
From monster's view, and all things shall be peace.
   Puck. My fairy lord, this must be done with haste,   395
For night's swift dragons cut the clouds full fast,

Neptune, god of the sea.
From R. Whitcombe, *Janua Divorum* . . . (1678).

400. That in crossways and floods have burial: that were buried without proper religious rites. Suicides were buried in crossways without such rites and the bodies of the drowned would necessarily lack them.

406. the Morning's love: Cephalus, beloved of Aurora, the goddess of morning; as related in Ovid's *Metamorphoses*, Book VII.

409. Neptune: that is, the ocean, Neptune's realm.

421. straight: immediately.

And yonder shines Aurora's harbinger,
At whose approach ghosts, wand'ring here and there,
Troop home to churchyards; damned spirits all,
That in crossways and floods have burial,   400
Already to their wormy beds are gone,
For fear lest day should look their shames upon,
They wilfully themselves exile from light,
And must for aye consort with black-browed night.
   Ob. But we are spirits of another sort.   405
I with the Morning's love have oft made sport,
And, like a forester, the groves may tread
Even till the eastern gate, all fiery red,
Opening on Neptune, with fair blessed beams
Turns into yellow gold his salt green streams.   410
But notwithstanding, haste, make no delay:
We may effect this business yet ere day.   [*Exit.*]
   Puck. Up and down, up and down,
      I will lead them up and down:
      I am feared in field and town.   415
      Goblin, lead them up and down.
Here comes one.

Enter *Lysander*.

   Lys. Where art thou, proud Demetrius? Speak thou
   now.
   Puck. Here, villain, drawn and ready. Where art thou? 420
   Lys. I will be with thee straight.
   Puck.   Follow me then
To plainer ground.
                    [*Exit Lysander.*]

429. **recreant**: coward. The original meaning was a person who broke faith, but in feudal times breaking faith with a man's lord in battle became equated with cowardice.

444. **Abide me**: wait for me; **wot**: know.

Enter *Demetrius*.

Dem.   Lysander, speak again!
Thou runaway, thou coward, art thou fled?   425
Speak! In some bush? Where dost thou hide thy head?
     Puck. Thou coward, art thou bragging to the stars,
Telling the bushes that thou look'st for wars,
And wilt not come? Come, recreant! come, thou child!
I'll whip thee with a rod. He is defiled   430
That draws a sword on thee.
     Dem.   Yea, art thou there?
     Puck. Follow my voice. We'll try no manhood here.
                                   Exeunt.

[Enter *Lysander*.]

Lys. He goes before me and still dares me on;
When I come where he calls, then he is gone.   435
The villain is much lighter-heeled than I.
I followed fast, but faster he did fly,
That fallen am I in dark uneven way,
And here will rest me. (*Lie down.*) Come, thou gentle
     day!   440
For if but once thou show me thy grey light,
I'll find Demetrius and revenge this spite.   [*Sleeps.*]

Enter *Puck* and *Demetrius*.

Puck. Ho, ho, ho! Coward, why com'st thou not?
     Dem. Abide me, if thou dar'st; for well I wot
Thou run'st before me, shifting every place,   445

454. **By day's approach look to be visited:** that is, don't expect me to attack now until daylight.

456. **Abate:** lessen.

And dar'st not stand nor look me in the face.
Where art thou now?
    Puck.   Come hither; I am here.
    Dem. Nay then, thou mock'st me. Thou shalt buy this
    dear   450
If ever I thy face by daylight see.
Now, go thy way: faintness constraineth me
To measure out my length on this cold bed.
By day's approach look to be visited.
                        [Lies down and sleeps.]

Enter *Helena*.

    Hel. O weary night, O long and tedious night,   455
Abate thy hours! Shine comforts from the East,
That I may back to Athens by daylight
From these that my poor company detest;
And sleep, that sometimes shuts up sorrow's eye,
Steal me awhile from mine own company.   *Sleep.* 460
    Puck.   Yet but three? Come one more:
            Two of both kinds makes up four.
            Here she comes, curst and sad.
            Cupid is a knavish lad
            Thus to make poor females mad.   465

Enter *Hermia*.

    Her. Never so weary, never so in woe;
Bedabbled with the dew, and torn with briers;
I can no further crawl, no further go;
My legs can keep no pace with my desires.

Here will I rest me till the break of day.   470
Heavens shield Lysander, if they mean a fray!
                              [*Lies down and sleeps.*]
   Puck.   On the ground
                Sleep sound.
                I'll apply
                To your eye,   475
    Gentle lover, remedy.
      [*Squeezes the herb on Lysander's eyelids.*]
                When thou wak'st,
                Thou tak'st
                True delight
                In the sight   480
Of thy former lady's eye;
And the country proverb known,
That every man should take his own,
In your waking shall be shown:
                Jack shall have Jill;   485
                Naught shall go ill;
The man shall have his mare again, and all shall be well.
                              [*Exit.*]

A
MIDSUMMER
NIGHT'S
DREAM

ACT IV

IV. [i.] Titania and her attendants wait upon Bottom. Oberon, accompanied by Puck, enters, just as the Fairy Queen and her adored fall asleep in each other's arms. Oberon has at last persuaded her to give up the boy and, in pity for her ridiculous plight, is ready to release her from the charm. He applies the antidote and Titania awakens with only a shadowy recollection of her enchantment. Bottom is restored to his normal state, and Titania and Oberon, reunited, dance together before exiting.

Theseus, Hippolyta, Egeus, and attendants, who have been performing May Day rites, enter and plan a hunt, until Theseus notices the four sleeping lovers, who are identified by Egeus and awakened by the huntsmen's horns. Demetrius and Lysander, questioned by Theseus about their presence, reveal what they can recall of the confused happenings of the night, and Theseus decrees that the two couples shall be married in company with himself and Hippolyta. Alone, Bottom also awakens, bemused, with a vague remembrance of his adventures, which he believes to have been a dream.

‖‖‖‖‖‖‖‖‖‖‖‖‖‖‖‖‖‖‖‖‖‖‖‖‖‖

2. **amiable:** lovable, lovely.
15-6. **overflowen with:** covered by; drowned.

ACT IV

[Scene I. The wood. Lysander, Demetrius, Helena,
and Hermia, all lying asleep.]

Enter [*Titania,*] *Queen of Fairies,* and [*Bottom the*]
Clown, and *Fairies,* [*Peaseblossom, Cobweb, Moth, Mustardseed,* and others]; and the *King,* [*Oberon,*] behind
them.

Tita. Come, sit thee down upon this flow'ry bed,
While I thy amiable cheeks do coy,
And stick musk-roses in thy sleek smooth head,
And kiss thy fair large ears, my gentle joy.

Bot. Where's Peaseblossom?   5

Peas. Ready.

Bot. Scratch my head, Peaseblossom. Where's
Mounsieur Cobweb?

Cob. Ready.

Bot. Mounsieur Cobweb, good mounsieur, get your   10
weapon in your hand, and kill me a red-hipped humble-
bee on the top of a thistle; and, good mounsieur, bring me
the honey-bag. Do not fret yourself too much in the
action, mounsieur; and, good mounsieur, have a care the
honey-bag break not. I would be loath to have you over-   15

Titania and Bottom.
Designed by Paul Konewka.

19. **neaf:** hand.

29. **the tongs and the bones:** primitive musical instruments used in country districts.

32. **bottle:** bundle.

33. **fellow:** equal.

38. **exposition:** a malapropism for "disposition."

40. **all ways away:** that is, spread yourselves to guard us from all sides.

42. **female ivy:** which clings like a wife to her husband.

flowen with a honey-bag, signior. Where's Mounsieur
Mustardseed?

Mus. Ready.

Bot. Give me your neaf, Mounsieur Mustardseed. Pray
you, leave your curtsy, good mounsieur.   20

Mus. What's your will?

Bot. Nothing, good mounsieur, but to help Cavalery
Peaseblossom to scratch. I must to the barber's, mounsieur;
for methinks I am marvelous hairy about the face; and
I am such a tender ass, if my hair do but tickle me, I must 25
scratch.

Tita. What, wilt thou hear some music, my sweet love?

Bot. I have a reasonable good ear in music. Let's have
the tongs and the bones.   *Music, tongs, rural music.*

Tita. Or say, sweet love, what thou desirest to eat.   30

Bot. Truly, a peck of provender. I could munch your
good dry oats. Methinks I have a great desire to a bottle of
hay: good hay, sweet hay, hath no fellow.

Tita. I have a venturous fairy that shall seek
The squirrel's hoard, and fetch thee new nuts.   35

Bot. I had rather have a handful or two of dried pease.
But I pray you, let none of your people stir me. I have an
exposition of sleep come upon me.

Tita. Sleep thou, and I will wind thee in my arms.
Fairies, be gone, and be all ways away.   40

                                        [*Exeunt Fairies.*]

So doth the woodbine the sweet honeysuckle
Gently entwist; the female ivy so
Enrings the barky fingers of the elm.
O, how I love thee! how I dote on thee!

                                        [*They sleep.*]

Diana.
From Cartari, *Imagini delli Dei de gl'Antichi* (1615).

48. **favors:** tokens of love.

52. **sometime:** formerly.

53. **orient:** radiant with the characteristic sheen of a pearl.

54. **flouriets':** little flowers'.

59. **straight:** at once; see III. [ii.] 421.

62. **imperfection:** error.

66. **repair:** betake themselves, go.

67. **accidents:** happenings.

.72. **Dian's bud:** the antidote to the passion-provoking herb. **Dian** is the chaste goddess Diana of classical mythology.

Enter [*Puck*,] *Robin Goodfellow.*

Ob. Welcome, good Robin. Seest thou this sweet sight?   45
Her dotage now I do begin to pity;
For, meeting her of late behind the wood,
Seeking sweet favors for this hateful fool,
I did upbraid her and fall out with her.
For she his hairy temples then had rounded   50
With coronet of fresh and fragrant flowers;
And that same dew which sometime on the buds
Was wont to swell like round and orient pearls
Stood now within the pretty flouriets' eyes,
Like tears that did their own disgrace bewail.   55
When I had at my pleasure taunted her,
And she in mild terms begged my patience,
I then did ask of her her changeling child;
Which straight she gave me, and her fairy sent
To bear him to my bower in fairyland.   60
And now I have the boy, I will undo
This hateful imperfection of her eyes.
And, gentle Puck, take this transformed scalp
From off the head of this Athenian swain;
That, he awaking when the other do,   65
May all to Athens back again repair,
And think no more of this night's accidents
But as the fierce vexation of a dream.
But first I will release the Fairy Queen.
          Be as thou wast wont to be;   70
          See as thou wast wont to see.
          Dian's bud o'er Cupid's flower
          Hath such force and blessed power.

Titania and Oberon reconciled.
Designed by Paul Konewka.

91. **solemnly**: ceremoniously.
92. **triumphantly**: with magnificent show.
98. **sad**: grave.

Now, my Titania! Wake you, my sweet queen.
  Tita. My Oberon, what visions have I seen!   75
Methought I was enamored of an ass.
  Ob. There lies your love.
  Tita.   How came these things to
    pass?
O, how mine eyes do loathe his visage now!   80
  Ob. Silence awhile. Robin, take off this head.
Titania, music call; and strike more dead
Than common sleep of all these five the sense.
  Tita. Music, ho, music! such as charmeth sleep!
  Puck. Now, when thou wak'st, with thine own fool's 85
    eyes peep.
  Ob. Sound, music! [*Music.*] Come, my queen, take
    hands with me.
And rock the ground whereon these sleepers be.
                        [*They dance.*]
Now thou and I are new in amity,   90
And will tomorrow midnight solemnly
Dance in Duke Theseus' house triumphantly
And bless it to all fair prosperity.
There shall the pairs of faithful lovers be
Wedded, with Theseus, all in jollity.   95
  Puck.   Fairy King, attend and mark.
           I do hear the morning lark.
  Ob.   Then, my queen, in silence sad
           Trip we after night's shade.
           We the globe can compass soon,   100
           Swifter than the wand'ring moon.
  Tita.   Come, my lord, and in our flight
           Tell me how it came this night

107. **observation:** that is, observance of May Day.

108. **vaward:** vanguard, the earliest part.

115. **Cadmus:** brother of Europa and founder of the city of Thebes in Greek mythology.

116. **bayed:** pursued with barking and brought to bay.

123. **flewed:** having folds of flesh about the mouth (like a bloodhound); **sanded:** sand-colored.

127. **Each under each:** that is, their voices varied in pitch with the effect of a scale of notes; **cry:** pack of hounds; **tuneable:** tuneful; see I. [i.] 187.

That I sleeping here was found
With these mortals on the ground.   105

[*Exeunt.*]

Wind horn.

Enter *Theseus* and all his *Train;* [*Hippolyta, Egeus*].

The. Go, one of you, find out the forester;
For now our observation is performed;
And since we have the vaward of the day,
My love shall hear the music of my hounds.
Uncouple in the western valley; let them go.   110
Dispatch, I say, and find the forester.

[*Exit an Attendant.*]

We will, fair Queen, up to the mountain's top
And mark the musical confusion
Of hounds and echo in conjunction.
Hip. I was with Hercules and Cadmus once   115
When in a wood of Crete they bayed the bear
With hounds of Sparta. Never did I hear
Such gallant chiding; for, besides the groves,
The skies, the fountains, every region near
Seemed all one mutual cry. I never heard   120
So musical a discord, such sweet thunder.
The. My hounds are bred out of the Spartan kind;
So flewed, so sanded; and their heads are hung
With ears that sweep away the morning dew;
Crook-kneed, and dew-lapped like Thessalian bulls;   125
Slow in pursuit, but matched in mouth like bells,
Each under each. A cry more tuneable
Was never holloaed to nor cheered with horn
In Crete, in Sparta, nor in Thessaly.

130. **soft:** hold on.
137. **grace:** honor.
148. **jealousy:** suspicion.

Judge when you hear. But, soft! What nymphs are these?   130
    Ege. My lord, this is my daughter here asleep;
And this, Lysander; this Demetrius is;
This Helena, old Nedar's Helena.
I wonder of their being here together.
    The. No doubt they rose up early to observe   135
The rite of May; and, hearing our intent,
Came here in grace of our solemnity.
But speak, Egeus. Is not this the day
That Hermia should give answer of her choice?
    Ege. It is, my lord.   140
    The. Go, bid the huntsmen wake them with their horns.
    [*Servant goes out.*] *Shout within. Wind horns. They*
                                        all start up.
Good morrow, friends. Saint Valentine is past.
Begin these woodbirds but to couple now?
    Lys. Pardon, my lord.
                                        [*They kneel.*]
    The.   I pray you all, stand up.   145
I know you two are rival enemies.
How comes this gentle concord in the world
That hatred is so far from jealousy
To sleep by hate and fear no enmity?
    Lys. My lord, I shall reply amazedly,   150
Half sleep, half waking; but as yet, I swear,
I cannot truly say how I came here;
But, as I think (for truly would I speak),
And now I do bethink me, so it is—
I came with Hermia hither. Our intent   155
Was to be gone from Athens, where we might,
Without the peril of the Athenian law—

167. **in fancy:** because of her love.
171. **gaud:** trinket; see I. [i.] 34.
173. **virtue:** power.
183. **overbear:** overrule.

Ege. Enough, enough, my lord! you have enough.
I beg the law, the law, upon his head.
They would have stol'n away; they would, Demetrius!   160
Thereby to have defeated you and me—
You of your wife, and me of my consent,
Of my consent that she should be your wife.

Dem. My lord, fair Helen told me of their stealth,
Of this their purpose hither, to this wood;   165
And I in fury hither followed them,
Fair Helena in fancy following me.
But, my good lord, I wot not by what power
(But by some power it is) my love to Hermia,
Melted as the snow, seems to me now   170
As the remembrance of an idle gaud
Which in my childhood I did dote upon;
And all the faith, the virtue of my heart,
The object and the pleasure of mine eye,
Is only Helena. To her, my lord,   175
Was I betrothed ere I saw Hermia;
But, like a sickness, did I loathe this food;
But, as in health, come to my natural taste,
Now I do wish it, love it, long for it,
And will for evermore be true to it.   180

The. Fair lovers, you are fortunately met.
Of this discourse we more will hear anon.
Egeus, I will overbear your will;
For in the temple, by-and-by, with us,
These couples shall eternally be knit;   185
And, for the morning now is something worn,
Our purposed hunting shall be set aside.
Away, with us to Athens! Three and three,

189. **solemnity:** ceremonious pomp.

197. **Mine own, and not mine own:** not certainly mine but likely to be taken by another with a prior claim.

213. **go about:** attempt.

215. **patched:** dressed in motley, such as professional fools wore.

216. **The eye of man, etc.:** Bottom's version of I Corinthians 2:9.

We'll hold a feast in great solemnity.
Come, Hippolyta.   190
     Exeunt Duke [*Theseus, Hippolyta, Egeus,*] *and
                       Lords.*

   Dem. These things seem small and undistinguishable,
Like far-off mountains turned into clouds.

   Her. Methinks I see these things with parted eye,
When everything seems double.

   Hel.   So methinks;   195
And I have found Demetrius like a jewel,
Mine own, and not mine own.

   Dem.   Are you sure
That we are awake? It seems to me
That yet we sleep, we dream. Do not you think   200
The duke was here, and bid us follow him?

   Her. Yea, and my father.

   Hel.   And Hippolyta.

   Lys. And he did bid us follow to the temple.

   Dem. Why then, we are awake. Let's follow him, 205
And by the way let us recount our dreams.

                         Exeunt.

   Bot. (Waking) When my cue comes, call me, and I will
answer. My next is "Most fair Pyramus." Hey-ho! Peter
Quince! Flute the bellows-mender! Snout the tinker!
Starveling! God's my life! Stol'n hence, and left me asleep! 210
I have had a most rare vision. I have had a dream, past
the wit of man to say what dream it was. Man is but an
ass if he go about to expound this dream. Methought I
was—there is no man can tell what. Methought I was, and
methought I had—But man is but a patched fool if he will 215
offer to say what methought I had. The eye of man hath

220. **ballet:** ballad.

━━━━━━━━━━━━━━━

IV. [ii.] Bottom's comrades are puzzling over his disappearance when he appears and urges them to prepare for their performance, which he is certain will be in demand at the duke's wedding.

━━━━━━━━━━━━━━━

3. **Out of doubt:** doubtless.

3-4. **transported:** carried to another world (by magic or a supernatural agent).

14. **a thing of naught:** a wicked thing.

not heard, the ear of man hath not seen, man's hand is
not able to taste, his tongue to conceive, nor his heart to
report what my dream was. I will get Peter Quince to
write a ballet of this dream. It shall be called "Bottom's   220
Dream," because it hath no bottom; and I will sing it in
the latter end of a play, before the duke. Peradventure, to
make it the more gracious, I shall sing it at her death.

Exit.

[Scene II. Athens. Quince's house.]

Enter *Quince, Flute, Snout,* and *Starveling.*

Quince. Have you sent to Bottom's house? Is he come
home yet?

Starv. He cannot be heard of. Out of doubt he is transported.

Flute. If he come not, then the play is marred; it goes   5
not forward, doth it?

Quince. It is not possible. You have not a man in all
Athens able to discharge Pyramus but he.

Flute. No, he hath simply the best wit of any handi-
craft man in Athens.   10

Quince. Yea, and the best person too, and he is a very
paramour for a sweet voice.

Flute. You must say "paragon." A paramour is (God
bless us!) a thing of naught.

23. **hearts:** men of spirit, hearties.

24. **courageous:** Quince may think this means "heartening."

27. **no true Athenian:** Bottom here again is garbling a Biblical passage: Acts 17:21.

28. **right:** exactly.

34. **preferred:** put forward.

Enter Snug the Joiner.

Snug. Masters, the duke is coming from the temple, 15
and there is two or three lords and ladies more married. If
our sport had gone forward, we had all been made men.

Flute. O sweet bully Bottom! Thus hath he lost sixpence a day during his life. He could not have scaped
sixpence a day. An the duke had not given him sixpence 20
a day for playing Pyramus, I'll be hanged! He would have
deserved it. Sixpence a day in Pyramus, or nothing!

Enter Bottom.

Bot. Where are these lads? Where are these hearts?
Quince. Bottom! O most courageous day! O most
happy hour! 25
Bot. Masters, I am to discourse wonders; but ask me
not what. For if I tell you, I am no true Athenian. I will
tell you everything, right as it fell out.
Quince. Let us hear, sweet Bottom.
Bot. Not a word of me. All that I will tell you is that 30
the duke hath dined. Get your apparel together, good
strings to your beards, new ribbands to your pumps; meet
presently at the palace; every man look o'er his part; for
the short and the long is, our play is preferred. In any
case, let Thisby have clean linen; and let not him that 35
plays the lion pare his nails, for they shall hang out for
the lion's claws. And, most dear actors, eat no onions nor
garlic, for we are to utter sweet breath; and I do not doubt
but to hear them say it is a sweet comedy. No more
words. Away! go, away! 40

Exeunt.

A
MIDSUMMER
NIGHT'S
DREAM

ACT V

V. [i.] The three pairs of lovers have been married and, given a choice of entertainment after supper, Theseus selects the interlude to be performed by Bottom and his friends. The rustics' bungling enactment of "Pyramus and Thisby" is comic rather than tragic and provides an amusing finale to an evening of delight.

━━━━━━━━━━━━━

3. **may:** can.

4. **antique:** fantastic; **toys:** whimsicalities.

6. **fantasies:** fancies; see I. [i.] 33.

9. **Are of imagination all compact:** are completely made up of imagination.

12. **a brow of Egypt:** a gypsy beauty.

15. **bodies forth:** gives physical shape to.

ACT V

[Scene I. Athens. The Palace of Theseus.]

Enter *Theseus*, *Hippolyta*, and *Philostrate*,
    [*Lords*, and other *Attendants*].

Hip. 'Tis strange, my Theseus, that these lovers speak
   of.
The. More strange than true. I never may believe
These antique fables nor these fairy toys.
Lovers and madmen have such seething brains,   5
Such shaping fantasies, that apprehend
More than cool reason ever comprehends.
The lunatic, the lover, and the poet,
Are of imagination all compact.
One sees more devils than vast hell can hold: 10
That is the madman. The lover, all as frantic,
Sees Helen's beauty in a brow of Egypt.
The poet's eye, in a fine frenzy rolling,
Doth glance from heaven to earth, from earth to heaven;
And as imagination bodies forth   15
The forms of things unknown, the poet's pen
Turns them to shapes, and gives to airy nothing
A local habitation and a name.
Such tricks hath strong imagination

20. **apprehend:** conceive.

21. **comprehends:** includes (in its conception); **some bringer of that joy:** some reason to be joyful.

24. **all the story:** the story in detail.

25. **all their minds transfigured so together:** the fact that all their minds suffered the same delusion.

26. **More witnesseth:** attests to more.

27. **grows to something of great constancy:** approaches a total effect of consistency.

28. **howsoever:** anyway; **admirable:** to be wondered at.

37. **after-supper:** dessert.

43. **abridgment:** pastime.

44. **beguile:** while away.

46. **brief:** list; **ripe:** ready.

That, if it would but apprehend some joy,   20
It comprehends some bringer of that joy;
Or in the night, imagining some fear,
How easy is a bush supposed a bear!
    Hip. But all the story of the night told over,
And all their minds transfigured so together,   25
More witnesseth than fancy's images
And grows to something of great constancy;
But howsoever, strange and admirable.

Enter Lovers—*Lysander, Demetrius, Hermia,* and *Helena.*

    The. Here come the lovers, full of joy and mirth.
Joy, gentle friends, joy and fresh days of love   30
Accompany your hearts!
    Lys.   More than to us
Wait in your royal walks, your board, your bed!
    The. Come now, what masques, what dances shall we
        have,   35
To wear away this long age of three hours
Between our after-supper and bedtime?
Where is our usual manager of mirth?
What revels are in hand? Is there no play
To ease the anguish of a torturing hour?   40
Call Philostrate.
    Phil.   Here, mighty Theseus.
    The. Say, what abridgment have you for this evening?
What masque? what music? How shall we beguile
The lazy time, if not with some delight?   45
    Phil. There is a brief how many sports are ripe.
Make choice of which your Highness will see first.
                                            [*Gives a paper.*]

48. **The battle with the Centaurs:** though Theseus himself took part in a battle with Centaurs, the reference to Hercules suggests that that hero's contest with them during his pursuit of the Erymanthian boar is the subject of the song. Plutarch's life of Theseus indicates that Hercules and Theseus were cousins.

Theseus battling with a centaur. From R. Whitcombe, *Janua Divorum* . . . (1678).

53. **the Thracian singer:** Orpheus, whose murder by the devotees of Bacchus is told by Ovid, *Metamorphoses,* Book XI.

56-7. **The thrice three Muses mourning for the death/ Of Learning, late deceased in beggary:** various attempts have been made to identify **Learning** as a contemporary Elizabethan figure, but none are convincing, and if Shakespeare intended a topical allusion it remains obscure.

59. **sorting with:** befitting.

78. **unbreathed:** unexercised, inexperienced.

The. "The battle with the Centaurs, to be sung
By an Athenian eunuch to the harp."
We'll none of that. That have I told my love   50
In glory of my kinsman Hercules.
"The riot of the tipsy Bacchanals,
Tearing the Thracian singer in their rage."
That is an old device, and it was played
When I from Thebes came last a conqueror.   55
"The thrice three Muses mourning for the death
Of Learning, late deceased in beggary."
That is some satire keen and critical,
Not sorting with a nuptial ceremony.
"A tedious brief scene of young Pyramus   60
And his love Thisby; very tragical mirth."
Merry and tragical? tedious and brief?
That is hot ice and wondrous strange snow.
How shall we find the concord of this discord?

Phil. A play there is, my lord, some ten words long, 65
Which is as brief as I have known a play;
But by ten words, my lord, it is too long,
Which makes it tedious; for in all the play
There is not one word apt, one player fitted.
And tragical, my noble lord, it is;   70
For Pyramus therein doth kill himself.
Which when I saw rehearsed, I must confess,
Made mine eyes water; but more merry tears
The passion of loud laughter never shed.

The. What are they that do play it?   75

Phil. Hard-handed men that work in Athens here,
Which never labored in their minds till now;
And now have toiled their unbreathed memories

"The thrice three Muses."
From Cartari, *Imagini delli Dei de gl'Antichi* (1615).

79. **against:** in preparation for; see III. [ii.] 100.

85. **Extremely stretched:** that is, their efforts have strained their abilities; **conned with cruel pain:** they have learned their lines with agonizing effort.

91. **wretchedness o'ercharged:** miserable folk taxed beyond their ability.

92. **duty in his service perishing:** duty destroying itself in the very act of performing its functions.

94. **in this kind:** of this sort.

97-8. **noble respect/ Takes it in might, not merit:** a generous estimate will make allowances for their failure in view of their attempting a task too difficult for them.

99. **come:** traveled; **clerks:** learned men.

103. **practiced accent:** rehearsed delivery.

107. **the modesty of fearful duty:** the shyness of one overawed by dutiful respect.

With this same play, against your nuptial.
  The. And we will hear it.   80
  Phil.   No, my noble lord;
It is not for you. I have heard it over,
And it is nothing, nothing in the world;
Unless you can find sport in their intents,
Extremely stretched and conned with cruel pain,   85
To do you service.
  The.   I will hear that play;
For never anything can be amiss
When simpleness and duty tender it.
Go bring them in; and take your places, ladies.   90
                          [Exit Philostrate.]
  Hip. I love not to see wretchedness o'ercharged,
And duty in his service perishing.
  The. Why, gentle sweet, you shall see no such thing.
  Hip. He says they can do nothing in this kind.
  The. The kinder we, to give them thanks for nothing. 95
Our sport shall be to take what they mistake;
And what poor duty cannot do, noble respect
Takes it in might, not merit.
Where I have come, great clerks have purposed
To greet me with premeditated welcomes;   100
Where I have seen them shiver and look pale,
Make periods in the midst of sentences,
Throttle their practiced accent in their fears,
And, in conclusion, dumbly have broke off,
Not paying me a welcome. Trust me, sweet,   105
Out of this silence yet I picked a welcome;
And in the modesty of fearful duty

111. **In least speak most:** are more eloquent the less they say; **capacity:** understanding.

112. **Prologue:** a Prologue was frequently used to explain the play or to give such other information as the audience might need; **addressed:** ready.

114-22. **If we offend . . . show:** The Prologue is deliberately mispunctuated for comic effect. Quince speaks his piece so that the meaning is distorted.

117. **end:** aim.

119. **as minding to content you:** with the intention of pleasing you.

124. **doth not stand upon points:** Shakespeare is punning here. Theseus means that Quince is unmindful of proper punctuation in reading the speech.

125. **rid:** ridden.

126. **stop:** period.

129. **recorder:** a woodwind instrument similar to a flute; **not in government:** undisciplined, uncontrolled.

I read as much as from the rattling tongue
Of saucy and audacious eloquence.
Love, therefore, and tongue-tied simplicity   110
In least speak most, to my capacity.

[Re-enter *Philostrate*.]

Phil. So please your Grace the Prologue is addressed.
The. Let him approach.   *Flourish trumpets.*

Enter the *Prologue (Quince).*

Pro. If we offend, it is with our good will.
That you should think, we come not to offend,   115
But with good will. To show our simple skill,
That is the true beginning of our end.
Consider then, we come but in despite.
We do not come, as minding to content you,
Our true intent is. All for your delight,   120
We are not here. That you should here repent you,
The actors are at hand: and, by their show,
You shall know all, that you are like to know.
The. This fellow doth not stand upon points.
Lys. He hath rid his prologue like a rough colt; he   125
knows not the stop. A good moral, my lord: it is not
enough to speak, but to speak true.
Hip. Indeed he hath played on his prologue like a child
on a recorder—a sound, but not in government.
The. His speech was like a tangled chain: nothing im-   130
paired, but all disordered. Who is next?

Wall.
Designed by Paul Konewka.

132. **Gentles**: gentlefolk, ladies and gentlemen.
144. **grisly**: gruesome; **hight**: is called.
149. **tall**: brave.
152. **broached**: stabbed.
156. **At large**: in full.

Enter *Pyramus* and *Thisby*, *Wall*, *Moonshine*, and *Lion*.

Pro. Gentles, perchance you wonder at this show;
But wonder on, till truth make all things plain.
This man is Pyramus, if you would know;
This beauteous lady Thisby is certain.   135
This man, with lime and roughcast, doth present
Wall, that vile Wall which did these lovers sunder;
And through Wall's chink, poor souls, they are content
To whisper. At the which let no man wonder.
This man, with lantern, dog, and bush of thorn,   140
Presenteth Moonshine. For, if you will know,
By moonshine did these lovers think no scorn
To meet at Ninus' tomb, there, there to woo.
This grisly beast, which Lion hight by name,
The trusty Thisby, coming first by night,   145
Did scare away, or rather did affright;
And as she fled, her mantle she did fall,
Which Lion vile with bloody mouth did stain.
Anon comes Pyramus, sweet youth and tall,
And finds his trusty Thisby's mantle slain;   150
Whereat, with blade, with bloody blameful blade,
He bravely broached his boiling bloody breast.
And Thisby, tarrying in mulberry shade,
His dagger drew, and died. For all the rest,
Let Lion, Moonshine, Wall, and lovers twain   155
At large discourse while here they do remain.
   The. I wonder if the lion be to speak.
   Dem. No wonder, my lord. One lion may, when many
asses do.

Exeunt [Prologue, Pyramus,] Lion,
Thisby, and Moonshine.

168. **right and sinister:** right and left; that is, horizontal.

186. **being sensible:** having feelings.

187. **again:** in return.

Bottom as Pyramus.
Designed by Paul Konewka.

Wall. In this same interlude it doth befall   160
That I, one Snout by name, present a wall;
And such a wall, as I would have you think,
That had in it a crannied hole or chink;
Through which the lovers, Pyramus and Thisby,
Did whisper often, very secretly.   165
This loam, this roughcast, and this stone doth show
That I am that same wall. The truth is so.
And this the cranny is, right and sinister,
Through which the fearful lovers are to whisper.
    The. Would you desire lime and hair to speak better? 170
    Dem. It is the wittiest partition that ever I heard discourse, my lord.

Enter *Pyramus*.

    The. Pyramus draws near the wall. Silence!
    Pyr. O grim-looked night! O night with hue so black!
O night, which ever art when day is not!   175
O night, O night! alack, alack, alack,
I fear my Thisby's promise is forgot!
And thou, O wall, O sweet, O lovely wall,
That stand'st between her father's ground and mine!
Thou wall, O wall, O sweet and lovely wall,   180
Show me thy chink, to blink through with mine eyne!
                    [*Wall holds up his fingers.*]
Thanks, courteous wall. Jove shield thee well for this!
But what see I? No Thisby do I see.
O wicked wall, through whom I see no bliss,
Cursed be thy stones for thus deceiving me!   185
    The. The wall, methinks, being sensible, should curse
again.

The three Fates: Clotho, Atropos, and Lachesis.
From Cartari, *Imagini delli Dei de gl'Antichi* (1587).

190. **fall pat**: come about precisely.

201. **Limander**: Leander, a Greek lover who nightly swam the Hellespont to visit his love, Hero.

202. **Helen**: presumably Hero is meant; Helen was not noted for her constancy.

203. **Shafalus . . . Procrus**: Cephalus and Procris, whose love story is told in Book VII of Ovid's *Metamorphoses*.

207. **Ninny's**: Ninus', as in l. 143.

208. **Tide**: betide; that is, happen.

Pyr. No, in truth, sir, he should not. "Deceiving me"
is Thisby's cue. She is to enter now, and I am to spy her
through the wall. You shall see it will fall pat as I told   190
you. Yonder she comes.

Enter *Thisby*.

This. O wall, full often hast thou heard my moans
For parting my fair Pyramus and me!
My cherry lips have often kissed thy stones,
Thy stones with lime and hair knit up in thee.   195
Pyr. I see a voice. Now will I to the chink,
To spy an I can hear my Thisby's face.
Thisby!
This. My love! thou art my love, I think.
Pyr. Think what thou wilt, I am thy lover's grace;   200
And, like Limander, am I trusty still.
This. And I, like Helen, till the Fates me kill.
Pyr. Not Shafalus to Procrus was so true.
This. As Shafalus to Procrus, I to you.
Pyr. O, kiss me through the hole of this vile wall!   205
This. I kiss the wall's hole, not your lips at all.
Pyr. Wilt thou at Ninny's tomb meet me straightway?
This. Tide life, tide death, I come without delay.
                        [*Exeunt Pyramus and Thisby.*]
Wall. Thus have I, Wall, my part discharged so;
And, being done, thus Wall away doth go.   *Exit.*   210
The. Now is the mural down between the two neigh-
bors.
Dem. No remedy, my lord, when walls are so wilful to
hear without warning.

216. **The best in this kind**: that is, the best of plays.

218. **your imagination then, and not theirs**: that is, appreciation must be based on the receptive imagination of the spectator rather than the imaginative performance of the actors.

227. **A lion-fell, nor else no lion's dam**: the skin of a lion only, not even a lioness in reality.

232. **a very fox for his valor**: more shrewd than valiant.

234-35. **his valor cannot carry his discretion**: his bravery does not exceed his discretion.

240. **horns on his head**: an old joke, implying that his wife has betrayed him.

Moonshine.
Designed by Paul Konewka.

Hip. This is the silliest stuff that ever I heard.   215

The. The best in this kind are but shadows; and the worst are no worse, if imagination amend them.

Hip. It must be your imagination then, and not theirs.

The. If we imagine no worse of them than they of themselves, they may pass for excellent men. Here come   220 two noble beasts in, a man and a lion.

Enter *Lion* and *Moonshine*.

Lion. You, ladies, you, whose gentle hearts do fear
The smallest monstrous mouse that creeps on floor,
May now perchance both quake and tremble here,
When lion rough in wildest rage doth roar.   225
Then know that I one Snug the joiner am,
A lion-fell, nor else no lion's dam;
For, if I should as lion come in strife
Into this place, 'twere pity on my life.

The. A very gentle beast, and of a good conscience.   230

Dem. The very best at a beast, my lord, that e'er I saw.

Lys. This lion is a very fox for his valor.

The. True; and a goose for his discretion.

Dem. Not so, my lord; for his valor cannot carry his discretion, and the fox carries the goose.   235

The. His discretion, I am sure, cannot carry his valor; for the goose carries not the fox. It is well. Leave it to his discretion, and let us listen to the moon.

Moon. This lantern doth the horned moon present—

Dem. He should have worn the horns on his head.   240

The. He is no crescent, and his horns are invisible within the circumference.

249. **snuff**: passion, with an obvious pun.

254. **stay**: await.

267. **moused**: the mantle has been treated by Lion in the way a cat handles a mouse.

Moon. This lantern doth the horned moon present.
Myself the man i' the moon do seem to be.

The. This is the greatest error of all the rest. The man 245
should be put into the lantern. How is it else the man i'
the moon?

Dem. He dares not come there for the candle; for, you
see, it is already in snuff.

Hip. I am aweary of this moon; would he would 250
change!

The. It appears, by his small light of discretion, that he
is in the wane; but yet, in courtesy, in all reason, we must
stay the time.

Lys. Proceed, Moon.   255

Moon. All that I have to say is to tell you that the
lantern is the moon; I, the man i' the moon; this thornbush, my thornbush; and this dog, my dog.

Dem. Why, all these should be in the lantern; for all
these are in the moon. But silence! Here comes Thisby. 260

Enter *Thisby*.

This. This is old Ninny's tomb. Where is my love?
Lion. O!   *The Lion roars. Thisby runs off.*
Dem. Well roared, Lion!
The. Well run, Thisby!
Hip. Well shone, Moon! Truly, the moon shines with a 265
good grace.   [*The Lion tears Thisby's mantle, and exit.*]
The. Well moused, Lion!
Dem. And then came Pyramus.
Lys. And so the Lion vanished.

The Furies.
From Cartari, *Imagini delli Dei de gl'Antichi* (1615).

272. **gleams:** Charles Knight's suggestion for "beams" in the early texts.

276. **dole:** sorrow.

282. **Furies:** three avenging deities in classical mythology; **fell:** deadly.

283. **Fates:** the three goddesses of classical mythology who determined human destiny. One spun the thread of life, another decided on its length, and a third cut it.

284. **thrum:** the unwoven end of thread in a woven fabric.

286. **passion:** great show of sorrow.

293. **confound:** destroy; see also **confounding,** III. [ii.] 94.

295. **pap:** nipple.

Enter *Pyramus*.

Pyr. Sweet moon, I thank thee for thy sunny beams;   270
I thank thee, moon, for shining now so bright;
For, by thy gracious, golden, glittering gleams,
I trust to take of truest Thisby sight.
        But stay! O spite!
        But mark, poor knight!   275
        What dreadful dole is here?
        Eyes, do you see?
        How can it be?
        O dainty duck! O dear!
        Thy mantle good,   280
        What, stained with blood?
        Approach, ye Furies fell!
        O Fates, come, come!
        Cut thread and thrum;
        Quail, crush, conclude, and quell!   285
The. This passion, and the death of a dear friend,
would go near to make a man look sad.
Hip. Beshrew my heart but I pity the man.
Pyr. O, wherefore, Nature, didst thou lions frame?
Since lion vile hath here deflow'red my dear;   290
Which is—no, no!—which was the fairest dame
That lived, that loved, that liked, that looked with cheer.
        Come, tears, confound!
        Out, sword, and wound
        The pap of Pyramus!   295
        Ay, that left pap
        Where heart doth hop.   [*Stabs himself.*]
        Thus die I, thus, thus, thus.
        Now am I dead,

Flute as Thisby.
Designed by Paul Konewka.

305. **die:** one of a pair of dice.
320. **means:** moans, laments; **videlicet:** to wit.

Now am I fled;   300
My soul is in the sky.
Tongue, lose thy light;
Moon, take thy flight.

> *[Exit Moonshine.]*

Now die, die, die, die, die!   *[Dies.]*

Dem. No die, but an ace, for him; for he is but one. 305

Lys. Less than an ace, man; for he is dead, he is
nothing.

The. With the help of a surgeon he might yet recover,
and yet prove an ass.

Hip. How chance Moonshine is gone before Thisby 310
comes back and finds her lover?

Enter *Thisby*.

The. She will find him by starlight. Here she comes;
and her passion ends the play.

Hip. Methinks she should not use a long one for such a
Pyramus. I hope she will be brief.   315

Dem. A mote will turn the balance, which Pyramus,
which Thisby, is the better; he for a man, God warrant
us!—she for a woman, God bless us!

Lys. She has spied him already with those sweet eyes.

Dem. And thus she means, videlicet: 320

This.   Asleep, my love?
               What, dead, my dove?
               O Pyramus, arise!
               Speak, speak! Quite dumb?
               Dead, dead? A tomb   325
               Must cover thy sweet eyes.
               These lily lips,

333. **Sisters Three:** another name for the Fates; see l. 283 above.

336. **gore:** blood.

337. **shore:** cut.

341. **imbrue:** stain (with blood).

349. **Bergomask dance:** a clownish dance, the name of which comes from the rustic inhabitants of Bergamo in Italy.

   This cherry nose,
   These yellow cowslip cheeks,
   Are gone, are gone.   330
   Lovers, make moan!
   His eyes were green as leeks.
    O Sisters Three,
    Come, come to me,
   With hands as pale as milk;   335
    Lay them in gore,
    Since you have shore
   With shears his thread of silk.
   Tongue, not a word!
   Come, trusty sword;   340
   Come, blade, my breast imbrue!
         [*Stabs herself.*]
   And farewell, friends.
   Thus Thisby ends.
   Adieu, adieu, adieu!   [*Dies.*]
The. Moonshine and Lion are left to bury the dead. 345
Dem. Ay, and Wall too.
Bot. [*Starts up*] No, I assure you; the wall is down that parted their fathers. Will it please you to see the Epilogue, or to hear a Bergomask dance between two of our company?   350
 The. No epilogue, I pray you; for your play needs no excuse. Never excuse; for when the players are all dead, there need none to be blamed. Marry, if he that writ it had played Pyramus and hanged himself in Thisby's garter, it would have been a fine tragedy; and so it is 355 truly, and very notably discharged. But, come, your Bergomask! Let your Epilogue alone.

          [*A dance.*]

"The triple Hecate."
From Cartari, *Imagini delli Dei de gl'Antichi* (1609).

361. **overwatched**: remained sleepless.

362. **palpable gross**: notably stupid.

367. **behowls**: Warburton's emendation of "beholds" in the early texts.

369. **fordone**: exhausted.

379. **triple Hecate**: the goddess called Diana in her earthly aspect, Phoebe in her aspect as the moon in the sky, and Hecate as a denizen of Hell and mistress of the supernatural activities of night.

382. **frolic**: gay.

The iron tongue of midnight hath told twelve.
Lovers, to bed; 'tis almost fairy time.
I fear we shall outsleep the coming morn   360
As much as we this night have overwatched.
This palpable gross play hath well beguiled
The heavy gait of night. Sweet friends, to bed.
A fortnight hold we this solemnity
In nightly revels and new jollity.   365

                                        Exeunt.

                Enter *Puck*, [with a broom].

Puck. Now the hungry lion roars,
         And the wolf behowls the moon;
         Whilst the heavy ploughman snores,
         All with weary task fordone.
         Now the wasted brands do glow,   370
         Whilst the screech owl, screeching loud,
         Puts the wretch that lies in woe
         In remembrance of a shroud.
         Now it is the time of night
         That the graves, all gaping wide,   375
         Every one lets forth his sprite,
         In the churchway paths to glide;
         And we fairies, that do run
         By the triple Hecate's team
         From the presence of the sun,   380
         Following darkness like a dream,
         Now are frolic. Not a mouse
         Shall disturb this hallowed house.
         I am sent, with broom, before,
         To sweep the dust behind the door.   385

400. **create:** created.
404. **blots of Nature's hand:** physical deformities.
410. **consecrate:** consecrated.

Enter *King* and *Queen of Fairies*, with all their *Train*.

   Ob.   Through the house give glimmering light,
           By the dead and drowsy fire;
           Every elf and fairy sprite
           Hop as light as bird from brier;
           And this ditty, after me,   390
           Sing, and dance it trippingly.
  Tita.   First rehearse your song by rote,
           To each word a warbling note.
           Hand in hand, with fairy grace,
           Will we sing, and bless this place.   395
                            [*Song and dance.*]
   Ob.   Now, until the break of day,
           Through this house each fairy stray.
           To the best bride-bed will we,
           Which by us shall blessed be;
           And the issue there create   400
           Ever shall be fortunate.
           So shall all the couples three
           Ever true in loving be;
           And the blots of Nature's hand
           Shall not in their issue stand;   405
           Never mole, harelip, nor scar,
           Nor mark prodigious, such as are
           Despised in nativity,
           Shall upon their children be.
           With this field-dew consecrate,   410
           Every fairy take his gait,
           And each several chamber bless,
           Through this palace, with sweet peace.

422. **idle:** foolish.

428. **serpent's tongue:** that is, hisses of displeasure from the audience.

And the owner of it blest
Ever shall in safety rest.   415
Trip away; make no stay;
Meet me all by break of day.

Exeunt [all but Puck].

Puck. If we shadows have offended,
Think but this, and all is mended—
That you have but slumb'red here   420
While these visions did appear.
And this weak and idle theme,
No more yielding but a dream,
Gentles, do not reprehend.
If you pardon, we will mend.   425
And, as I am an honest Puck,
If we have unearned luck
Now to scape the serpent's tongue,
We will make amends ere long;
Else the Puck a liar call.   430
So, good night unto you all.
Give me your hands, if we be friends,
And Robin shall restore amends.

[Exit.]

KEY TO
Famous Lines and Phrases

The course of true love never did run smooth
[Lysander—I. i. 136]

Over hill, over dale . . .   [Fairy—II. i. 2 ff.]

Ill met by moonlight, proud Titania.   [Oberon—II. i. 61]

. . . a fair Vestal, throned by the West   [Oberon—II. i. 161]

In maiden meditation, fancy-free   [Oberon—II. i. 167]

I'll put a girdle round about the earth   [Puck—II. i. 178]

I know a bank where the wild thyme blows
[Oberon—II. i. 254]

You spotted snakes with double tongue . . .
[1st Fairy—II. ii. 9 ff.]

Lord, what fools these mortals be!   [Puck—III. ii. 116]

I was with Hercules and Cadmus once
When in a wood of Crete they bayed the bear . . .
[Hippolyta—IV. i. 115-6]

The lunatic, the lover, and the poet,
Are of imagination all compact.   [Theseus—V. i. 8-9]

The lover . . .
Sees Helen's beauty in a brow of Egypt. [Theseus—V. i. 11-2]